Cryptocurrencies - Financial Technologies of the Future

Edited by Ireneusz Miciuła

Published in London, United Kingdom

Cryptocurrencies - Financial Technologies of the Future
http://dx.doi.org/10.5772/intechopen.105636
Edited by Ireneusz Miciuła

Contributors
Artina Bedjeti Baftijari, Delson Chikobvu, Eric Lambourdière, Ireneusz Miciuła, Jérôme Verny, Kiran Pingali, Lawrence Henesey, Leonid Nakov, Leslie Rodríguez-Valencia, Pavlo Parkhomenko, Prosper Lamothe-Fernández, Prosper Lamothe-López, Providence Mushori, Stanislaw P. Stawicki, Stephane Fourneaux, Thabani Ndlovu, Volodymyr Tkach, Yacine Aiat

First published in London, United Kingdom, 2024 by IntechOpen
IntechOpen is the global imprint of INTECHOPEN LIMITED, registered in England and Wales, registration number: 11086078, 167-169 Great Portland Street, London, W1W 5PF, United Kingdom

British Library Cataloguing-in-Publication Data
A catalogue record for this book is available from the British Library

Additional hard and PDF copies can be obtained from orders@intechopen.com

Cryptocurrencies - Financial Technologies of the Future
Edited by Ireneusz Miciuła
p. cm.
Print ISBN 978-0-85466-218-0
Online ISBN 978-0-85466-217-3
eBook (PDF) ISBN 978-0-85466-219-7

For EU product safety concerns:
IN TECH d.o.o., Prolaz Marije Krucifikse Kozulić 3, 51000 Rijeka, Croatia,
info@intechopen.com or visit our website at intechopen.com.

Meet the editor

Ireneusz Miciuła is an assistant professor at the Institute of Economics and Finance, University of Szczecin, Poland. He is the author of more than 250 scientific and journal publications in economics, finance, management, and IT. He has participated in many international scientific conferences. He was awarded a scholarship from the Human Capital Operational Program and participated three times in summer research at the European University Institute in Florence. He has served as a visiting researcher at many universities in Germany, Czech Republic, Romania, Albania, Greece, and Portugal. He is a member of the *Journal of Economics and Public Finance* and a reviewer for the Polish-US Fulbright Foundation. He is also a member of the Polish Finance and Banking Association and Polish Economic Society. He is an expert at the Polish Agency for Enterprise Development and the Energy Regulatory Office and a scientific expert at the Foundation for Polish Science.

Contents

Preface

Cryptocurrencies – Financial Technologies of the Future provides knowledge, recommendations, and practical solutions to new challenges within the contemporary processes of globalization and international trade thanks to cryptocurrencies.

This book explores all the processes involved in cryptocurrencies. Money is a fundamental payment element of the economy, and this book examines the role, importance, and benefits of introducing cryptocurrency as a new means of economic exchange. It describes the legal possibilities of integrating cryptocurrencies into payment systems, analyzes their benefits and risks, and assesses their development prospects and economic implications.

In today's global marketplace, financial phenomena are crucial, with ITC technology and financial flow regulations driving important changes. Cryptocurrencies are a key topic in this context, warranting ongoing exploration and establishment of operational principles. This book aims to address current topics related to social conditions and technical solutions, providing both theoretical insights and practical solutions concerning the functioning of cryptocurrencies in society.

Digital finance, often referred to as financial technology (FinTech), is the application of digital technologies to financial activities. The increasing use of digital financial services by consumers and businesses highlights the need for financial education across societies. The digital transformation of financial services and the rise of cryptocurrencies necessitate changes in global financial markets.

Cryptocurrencies – Financial Technologies of the Future presents comprehensive knowledge, current considerations, and practical solutions in financial science, focusing on cryptocurrencies as a new form of money. We would like to thank everyone who contributed to this publication, especially the authors for their inspiring scientific considerations. As the editor, I hope that this book will spark interest in the subject and inspire new solutions to the research problems discussed.

Ireneusz Miciuła
Department of Sustainable Finance and Capital Markets,
Institute of Economics and Finance,
University of Szczecin,
Szczecin, Poland

Chapter 1

Introductory Chapter: Cryptocurrencies as Financial Technologies of the Future

Ireneusz Miciuła

1. Introduction

Money is undoubtedly the basic payment element in the economy. Therefore, the history of money is also a picture of changes in financial markets [1]. We are currently witnessing technological changes in making payments in the economy. Therefore, we observe the importance and benefits of the possibility of introducing a new means of economic exchange. Cryptocurrencies may become one of the means of payment in the history of the world. There will certainly be changes in financial markets, with more possible payment methods. However, the form in which this will take place is currently being clarified, among other things, by the need to determine the legal standards that will apply to this development of financial resources. And financial phenomena are crucial in today's global market because ITC technology and the rules of financial flows are the most important changes in the modern global economy. Therefore, many current topics concern cryptocurrencies, which are extremely important and require constant discovery and determination of the principles of operation. This is related to the risks of introducing new forms of payment and the desire to highlight all the benefits that will support this innovative form of transaction in the economy. The development prospects of cryptocurrencies are undoubtedly the next milestone among forms of money, which has huge implications for the world's economies.

Thanks to the use of modern technology, cryptocurrencies are a kind of financial innovation (another milestone in the history of money) that has a chance to influence the global financial system. Cryptocurrencies are electronic money that does not require an intermediary, such as a bank, to complete the transaction. Thanks to this, the transaction and its parties are completely anonymous to the financial system controlled by global institutions. On the one hand, it provides enormous benefits by preventing global institutions from controlling and influencing world transactions. On the other hand, it does not provide an adequate level of security. Therefore, once the legal issues are settled and security is improved, it will be possible to use the advantages of this form of payment. Namely, it will allow us to speed up the settlement of payment transactions and thus become independent from traditional forms of payment and the restrictive control of global financial institutions.

Cryptocurrencies are an innovative and technologically advanced alternative to a fully globalized future. They can be an alternative to processing payments made across geographical borders [2]. Additionally, if cryptocurrencies are effectively

 IntechOpen

regulated through current adjustments, they will be able to help future generations meet the challenges of financial transactions in various forms. Cryptocurrencies perform the same functions as traditional money because they have features such as durability, divisibility, and originality, which, if socially accepted, will mean that they can be a full-fledged means of exchange. Over the last dozen or so years, cryptocurrencies have been gaining popularity, and their importance in financial markets is increasing [3]. The innovative nature of cryptocurrencies for society may prove to be something that will force changes and will have a huge impact on the functioning of the global financial sector in the future.

Cryptocurrencies are already recognized as an innovative payment method [4]. Currently, they are only complementary to official currencies. They do not generally have the legal status of a means of payment, but the number of transactions using them is growing. The number of service and commercial points accepting cryptocurrencies as a payment method is also increasing. The adaptation of commercial establishments to payments in cryptocurrencies is constantly growing. Therefore, this technology, with certain legal regulations, will undoubtedly have a huge impact on changes in the functioning of financial markets in global economies.

2. Cryptocurrencies: the definition of financial innovation

Finance is monetary resources, operations, and legal norms relating to them. Finance is also a social relationship that arises from collecting and spending money. Therefore, the science of finance examines money streams flowing between economic entities during the processes of production, distribution and exchange (consumption), and material accumulation, as well as money resources collected and distributed during these processes [5]. Finance is a field of science that deals with the analysis of how people allocate available financial resources in a given period, or it should be defined as all economic phenomena related to the accumulation and distribution of monetary resources, which can be defined as economic relations resulting from the movement of money, with the collection and spending of monetary resources [6]. Defining cryptocurrencies is a big challenge and may lead to inconsistencies in terms of economic sense and legal aspects.

The history of the concept's evolution can be seen in the literature due to its continuous development. Thanks to this, digital means of exchange are classified. The first concept refers to a virtual currency, which is a means of payment not issued by any financial institution (e.g., a bank), while also being a means of exchange of value between the issuer and the user. However, they operate within strictly defined limits and are used only to purchase virtual goods and services. Therefore, virtual currency in this understanding is presented in a narrow scope and mainly concerns virtual currencies that appear in mass online games. This approach proves that these currencies are not intended for the purchase of real tangible items but for the purchase of virtual goods or services that can only exist in the area of a limited virtual world [7]. Therefore, the term digital currency is a broader concept and refers to a means of payment in a specific jurisdiction in the conventional sense [8]. Currently, there is a separation of concepts and a desire to specify the full definition for cryptocurrencies. It seems that this will only happen when legal regulations are established and when they are applied in practice on a large scale.

Legal regulations in different European countries are different, or there are no regulations at all in relation to cryptocurrencies [9]. This may lead to inconsistencies and difficulties in the exchange of goods and services, as well as a lack of trading certainty. In 2015, the European Central Bank provided the following definition of a virtual currency: a digital representation of values that are not issued by a central bank, electronic money institution, or credit institution, which in certain conditions can be used as an alternative to money [10]. In its resolution of 26 May 2016 on virtual currencies, the European Parliament adopted that virtual currency is a synonym for digital cash that is not issued by a central bank or any public authority and is not linked to fiat currency but is used by natural or legal persons as a medium of exchange that can be transmitted, stored, and thus subjected to electronic trading [11]. Referring to the technology by which cryptocurrencies are created, which may also be called cryptocurrencies, they are defined as an accounting system based on cryptography whose characteristic feature is its dispersion [12]. This system is responsible for storing messages related to the ownership status in conventional units. The ownership status is linked to individual nodes of the so-called system—wallets, in such a way that only a person who has a specific and private key can control this wallet; a situation in which it would be issued twice to the same entity is impossible [13]. S. Nakamoto, the creator of bitcoin—the most popular cryptocurrency, defines it as an electronic coin in the form of a chain of digital signatures. Each holder of the coin transfers it to the next one, digitally signing the "hash" of the previous transaction and the public key of the next holder, adding them to the end of the coin. The recipient can verify the signatures to verify the chain of ownership [14]. This feature offers great opportunities to improve the security of financial transactions and to regulate legal solutions that will ensure full trust in this technology and influence changes in the global information society.

3. Financial technology (FinTech) era

Nowadays, running a business or investment activity requires the ability to search, analyze, and use selected information to support decision-making processes. A special role in obtaining information about economic entities is assigned to financial statements, which should provide useful financial information. This is why financial information is so fundamental in the information society. Especially since new information technologies are rapidly developing and being used in this field, the world has designated a new area of interest under the term financial technology (FinTech).

Digital finance, often referred to as financial technology (FinTech), is the application of digital technologies to financial activities [15]. Consumers and businesses are increasingly using digital financial services [16]. We are currently witnessing the digital transformation of financial services, which additionally increases the need for financial education of entire societies [17]. The digital revolution of the financial system along with the development of cryptocurrencies requires changes in the functioning of global financial markets.

The ongoing globalization of the world economy and the increasing number of free trade zones along with the simplification of trade processes are factors that facilitate the rapid implementation of trade contracts [18]. The demand for a fast, cheap, and functional trading system continues to grow. The use of cryptocurrency settlements may be particularly beneficial in global financial markets [19]. European Union authorities are working on new regulations that are intended to increase the potential of cryptocurrencies and reduce the risks associated with them (e.g., regulation on markets for cryptoassets - MiCA). MEPs reviewed and introduced changes to the draft prepared by the European Commission, and in March 2022, they decided to start negotiations on the final shape of these regulations with EU countries in the Council. To encourage development and use of these technologies, the new regulations are intended to ensure legal certainty and support innovation, consumer and investor protection, and financial stability [20]. The regulations also include provisions on transparency, disclosure of information, and authorization and supervision of transactions. The most common opinions regarding cryptocurrencies are that virtual currencies will be a new stage of development in the world's financial markets. However, certain solutions and regulations need to be developed, possibly based on trust in international institutions, which will result in shifting the likelihood of using the advantages and possibilities of using cryptocurrencies toward the development of the information society, thereby limiting possible crimes.

The aim of the book "Cryptocurrencies - Financial Technologies of the Future" will be to present knowledge, current considerations, and practical solutions in the field of broadly understood financial science and in particular the new form of money, which is cryptocurrencies. We would like to thank everyone who contributed to the creation of this publication, especially the authors, for their inspiring scientific considerations. As the editor of this monograph, I hope that many of the issues presented will motivate the reader to become interested in the subject, which will translate into new solutions to the research problems raised.

Author details

Ireneusz Miciuła
Department of Sustainable Finance and Capital Markets, Institute of Economics and Finance, University of Szczecin, Szczecin, Poland

*Address all correspondence to: irekmic@wp.pl

References

[1] Filar D, Łukasiewicz-Kamińska A, Miciuła I, Sobiecki G, Niedzwiecki A, Rakoczy J. Od muszli po Bitmonety. Oblicza pieniądza i systemów walutowych. Warszawa: Texter; 2014

[2] Abram G, Szymura T. Bitcoin – Still Cryptocurrency or Currency? 2024. Available from: http://www.infor.pl/Bitcoin-yet-cryptowaluta-czy-juz-waluta.html#ftn16

[3] Miciula I, Kadlubek M, Stępień P. Modern methods of business valuation—Case study and new concepts. Sustainability. 2020;**12**:2699. DOI: 10.3390/su12072699

[4] Augustyn D. How does a cryptocurrency exchange work? 2024. Available from: https://www.fxmag.pl/artykul/how-does-the-cryptocurrency-exchange-work

[5] Miciuła I. The concept of FTS analysis in forecasting trends of exchange rate changes. Economics & Sociology. 2014;**2**(7):172-182

[6] Beck T, Demirgüç-Kunt A, Levine R, Maksimovic V, Financial Structure and Economic Development. Firm, Industry, and Country Evidence, Policy Research Working Paper, Nr 2423. Washington, DC: The World Bank; 2000

[7] Ryfa J. Waluty wirtualne – problem zdefiniowania i klasyfikacji nowego środka płatniczego. Nauki o Finansach. 2014;**2**(19):138-147

[8] Ślażyńska-Kluczek D, Kazanecka K. Cryptocurriencies in the perspective of young poles. Myśl Ekonomiczna i Polityczna. 2022;**4**(75):69-88. DOI: 10.26399/meip.4(75).2022.23/d.slazynska-kluczek/k.kazanecka

[9] European Banking Authority, Opinion on virtual currencies. 2024. Available from: https://www.eba.europa.eu/documents/10180/657547/EBA-Op-2014-08+Opinion+on+Virtual+Currencies.pdf

[10] European Central Bank. Virtual Currency Schemes – a further analysis, Frankfurt am Main: European Central Bank. 2015. Available from: https://www.ecb.europa.eu/pub/pdf/other/virtualcurrencyschemesen.pdf, 17.05.2024

[11] European Parliament. 2016. Rezolucja Parlamentu Europejskiego z 26 maja 2016 r. w sprawie wirtualnych walut (2016/2007(INI))

[12] Ślażyńska-Kluczek D. Kryptoaktywa – podejście kluczowych regulatorów europejskich. Nauki Ekonomiczne. 2022;**35**:103-113

[13] Miciuła I. Global development and prospects for the implementation of cryptocurrencies and the state of this market in Poland. In: Czerwińska T, Nowak AZ, editors. Capital Market - Savings and Investments. Warszawa: WZ UW; 2019. p. 156

[14] Nakamoto S. Bitcoin: A peer-to-peer electronic cash system. 2024. Available from: https://bitcoin.org/bitcoin.pdf

[15] Vasek M, Moore T. There's no free lunch, even using bitcoin: Tracking the popularity and profits of virtual currency scams. In: International Conference on Financial Cryptography and Data Security. Berlin: Springer; 2015. pp. 44-61

[16] Yen K-C, Cheng H-P. Economic policy uncertainty and cryptocurrency volatility. Finance Research Letters. 2021;**38**:101428

[17] Miciuła I, Kazojć K. The global development of cryptocurrencies. Prace Naukowe Uniwersytetu Ekonomicznego we Wrocławiu. 2019;**63**(2):183-196. Available from: https://journals.ue.wroc.pl/pn/article/view/355

[18] Miciuła I. Financial innovations on the currency market as new instruments to risk management. Journal of International Studies. 2015;**1**(8):138-149

[19] Woebbeking F. Cryptocurrency volatility markets. Digital Finance. 2021;**3**(3):273-298

[20] Skelnik K, Miciuła I, Łubiński P. Zarządzanie bezpieczeństwem informacji. In: Metodyka, Ideologia, Państwo. Katowice: Wydawnictwo Nauka i Biznes; 2018

Chapter 2

Origins, Theoretical Foundations, and Economic Implications of Cryptocurrencies

Jérôme Verny, Yacine Aiat, Stephane Fourneaux and Eric Lambourdière

Abstract

The theoretical foundations and indeed implications related to the emergence of digital assets, particularly cryptocurrencies, remain a scarcely explored area in recent academic literature. This chapter aims to analyze the presumed influences of various economic schools of thought on the genesis of Bitcoin, the monetary policies underlying several digital assets, and the evolution of their market capitalization since 2009. The study also addresses the case of several cryptocurrency exchange platforms, commonly known as crypto exchanges, and focuses on industrial entities, such as Ledger and Bitmain. An overview of use cases involving "smart contracts" and Blockchain technology is provided. This chapter seeks to revisit the emergence of different approaches to national regulation on a global scale and to establish international comparisons. The examples of Japan, long trapped in a deflationary spiral, and Argentina, facing hyperinflation, are particularly enlightening for understanding the legal treatment of digital assets and their perception by local authorities. Two central questions guide this exploration: what are the economic and ideological foundations underlying the conception of Bitcoin, and to what extent does the current development of the digital asset ecosystem remain true to the initial ideas of Satoshi Nakamoto?

Keywords: cryptocurrencies, stablecoins, fiat money, real assets, digital assets, tokens, smart contracts, Blockchain, exchange, supply chain

1. Introduction

The financial crisis (2007–2008) and the massive adoption of new information and communication technologies (NICTs) have created a favorable environment for innovation[1]. In this context, the Blockchain and Bitcoin emerged, providing a solu-

[1] A digital asset commonly referred to as a cryptocurrency does not meet the established criteria of a currency since it lacks the backing of a Central Regulatory Body and is not acknowledged as official legal tender for settling all types of debts and transactions. Moreover, its significant fluctuations in price undermine its ability to serve as a consistent store of value and a reliable measure for pricing goods and services, which are fundamental attributes of conventional currencies.

tion to double spending while introducing a single consensus mechanism. Indeed, the Blockchain has been one of the most important technological and technical innovations in recent years. In his paper on Bitcoin "a peer-to-peer electronic system,"Satoshi Nakamoto explains the use and the structure of this new system. The abstract of the paper explained the direct online payment from one source to another source without relying on a third-party source. The paper describes an electronic payment system based on the concept of cryptography. Nakamoto's paper offered a solution to double spending, where a digital currency cannot be duplicated and spent more than once. The concept of a public ledger is introduced, where an electronic coin's transaction history can be traced and confirmed if the coin has not been spent before, preventing the problem of double spending.

This new movement has evolved very rapidly, bringing with it new cryptocurrencies (presented as a better alternative to Bitcoin) and new concepts. In 2014, the arrival of Ethereum and smart contracts ushered in a new era for crypto-assets. The concept of decentralized applications, decentralized finance, and the explosion of ICOs have fundamentally changed our ecosystem. The purpose of this chapter is to present the origin and functioning of Blockchain, as well as its practical use in the industrial world. In addition, the development of this new technology has raised many questions from governments as to how it should be regulated. This important factor in the regulation of Blockchain will be analyzed through a comparative study between European countries, Japan, Canada, and the BRICS group. The transparent and decentralized platform of the Blockchain has attracted different types of industries, and organizations are increasingly moving toward the use of the Blockchain for various business purposes. An example is the employment of the Blockchain in the supply chain industry. Even if the Blockchain adoption in the supply chain industry is still something recent, studies have been conducted, indicating the Blockchain's potential impact on supply chains. In the latest literature on supply chain operations, researchers and professionals claim that Blockchain can offer real-time transparency in the shipping industry among stakeholders such as port authorities, customs, and freight forwarders. The Blockchain provides a framework with secure data sharing, forecast, and risk analysis functions. According to Bocek et al. [1], smart contracts can decrease the number of intermediaries and allow for further automation in the supply chain process. Smart contracts can also cut operational costs. Pan [2] indicates that Blockchain technology can improve also information sharing between the supply chain stakeholders.

The use of Blockchain and, by implication, Bitcoin, has turned several industries in the global economy upside down, representing a major revolution in terms of regulation. Several financial institutions and organizations are now exploring different approaches to managing this new technology in the most efficient possible way. This chapter explores and presents the points of convergence and divergence regarding the regulations undertaken by the European Union countries, Japan, and the BRICS about the use of the Blockchain. To analyze and present the Blockchain, its challenges, its industrial applications, and the different regulatory approaches, this chapter is structured into four main sections. The rest of this section ends with a presentation of the origins and rise of Blockchain, and how it stands in comparison with the main economic theories. The second section covers the use of the Blockchain and smart contracts in the industrial world with a focus on the supply chain. The third section presents the different regulatory approaches taken by the countries considered in the analysis. Finally, the book chapter concludes with a fourth section dedicated to summarizing key findings and presenting conclusions.

1.1 Origins of the Blockchain

The 1970s and 1980s marked the beginning of two major phenomena that profoundly transformed societies worldwide: the liberalization of the economy and international financial markets and the rapid development of ICTs. The rise of new technologies accelerated sharply in the 1990s with the development of the Internet, then in the early 2000s with the advent of the smartphone and social networking. This enabled people to access computing power and data processing capabilities from their own homes. Consequently, these changes have introduced unprecedented challenges, particularly in terms of the role of the state, the protection of privacy, and respect for individual freedoms.

Moreover, the 2008 financial crisis has created favorable conditions for the emergence of new alternatives to the traditional monetary and financial system. This dynamic context has led to the emergence of Bitcoin, creating an opportunity for innovations likely to provide more transparent, secure, and decentralized solutions. This event led to the reintroduction of decentralized and secure concepts, such as those outlined in Satoshi Nakamoto's white paper. Published at the peak of the crisis to a private list of cryptographers on October 31, 2008, the eight-page white paper entitled "Bitcoin: a peer-to-peer electronic payment system" describes the technical foundations of Bitcoin [3]. Indeed, Bitcoin represents one of the most popular Blockchain technologies that hosts a digital ledger. Bitcoin provides the platform to mine, store, and trade Bitcoins *via* a complex computer algorithm that is tied to a distributed network [4]. In the traditional financial system, banks and other financial institutions solve the double-spending issue by keeping centralized records of transactions and checking each transaction against this record to ensure that a unit of currency is only spent once. However, Satoshi Nakamoto, a supporter of the cypherpunk movement, did not want to rely on a central entity that was vulnerable to attack, expensive to run, and likely to delay transactions. To avoid this problem, Nakamoto proposed a decentralized solution where all transactions are broadcast and recorded on a "public ledger" called the Blockchain, and where participants can agree on a single transaction order history. In other words, the Blockchain can be defined as a database of records of transactions that are distributed, maintained, and validated by a network of computers worldwide. Records are controlled by a large community, and no single person has control over them, making it impossible to modify or delete a transaction's history. Each time, a person makes a transaction, it is transmitted to the network, and computer algorithms verify its authenticity. Once the transaction has been verified, this new transaction is then linked to the previous one to form a chain of transactions. And that is how it is called Blockchain, such as explain by Lambourdiere & al. [5].

Thus, Wamba & Queiroz define the Blockchain as a shared (distributed) and decentralized ledger. This is probably the biggest idea behind Blockchain. It is the idea that distinguishes it from databases or regular ledgers. Moreover, not all the Blockchains have the same characteristics. Two types of Blockchains exist, the "permissioned" and "permissionless" [6]. With permissionless Blockchains, anyone can participate. This is the case with Bitcoin and Ethereum, two cryptocurrencies that any individual can participate in and trade. Permissionless Blockchains are in theory more secure as there are more ledgers to confirm or deny claims. These types of Blockchains are also subject to malicious actors being able to enter the network and wreak havoc as they are more exposed and have no vetting process (**Figure 1**).

In complement to the security that comes from the distributed ledger, Blockchain technology also uses cryptography to add a higher level of security. The emergence

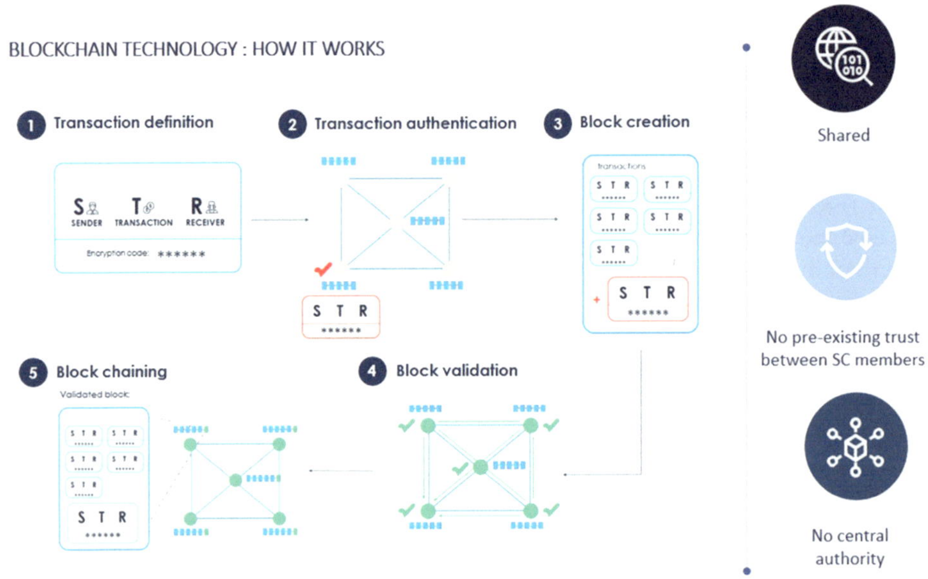

Figure 1.
Presentation of the Blockchain technology. Source: [5].

of Blockchain, thus, marked a decisive milestone in the pursuit of a decentralized system free from the constraints of traditional financial institutions. The architecture of Blockchain, combined with an innovative approach to confidentiality and game theory, has made it possible to solve several challenges and to achieve significant notoriety. Following the success of Bitcoin, an increasing number of developers became interested in the potential benefits of Blockchain and sought to improve, diversify, or simply imitate the Bitcoin proposition.

The year 2011 witnessed the arrival of the first Altcoins (i.e. tokens other than Bitcoin). The rise of Altcoins, with their different approaches and innovations, has highlighted the diversity and flexibility of Blockchain technology. Although Bitcoin was the pioneer and remains the best-known digital asset, Altcoins have introduced varied ideas and solutions for existing problems and explored new use cases. These new currencies have attracted growing interest, creating a need for investors and users to trade them efficiently, securely, and conveniently. In this context, the first centralized crypto exchanges of asset emerged, offering a platform to buy, sell, and trade various digital currencies. With the proliferation of crypto-assets, a mechanism to facilitate their trade quickly became a critical necessity. While the original philosophy of digital assets emphasized decentralization, a distortion has become apparent in the development of centralized institutions to facilitate their exchange. Centralized exchanges for crypto- assets, often referred to as "exchanges," operate as intermediaries, bringing buyers and sellers together under a single virtual roof. Unlike peer-to-peer systems, where transactions are direct between users, a centralized exchange functions as a trusted third party. Users deposit their assets on the platform, and the platform ensures that bids and ask prices are matched, facilitates transactions, and maintains an internal ledger. The growth of Bitcoin's price from negligible value to several thousand dollars in just a few years demonstrates its growing adoption and recognition as a potential investment asset worldwide. Altcoins have followed, each with its innovations and solutions to the challenges presented in Bitcoin.

1.2 The theoretical foundation of the Blockchain

The reference to the gold standard brings to mind the link between the classical theory of the late nineteenth century and Bitcoin. The comparison between proof-of-work and the gold standard is often made by many developers, professionals, and observers of the digital asset industry, who also refer to Bitcoin as "digital gold." The terminology used by Satoshi to define the role of those in charge of the network's security (the "miners") may refer to the energy-intensive activity of mining. Bitcoins, such as gold, exist in limited quantities, which no state or entity can control. However, a debate remains over Bitcoin's intrinsic value, which can be resolved by admitting that the intrinsic value of a Bitcoin is at least equivalent to the average cost of the energy used to secure the network. Finally, it is by looking at the criticisms made by neoclassical economists regarding the gold standard and those made today about Bitcoin that we can observe some common features between the systems:

- Both systems lack monetary flexibility: Under the gold standard, a country's monetary policy is closely tied to its gold reserves. This limits the ability of central banks to adjust the money supply to meet economic needs, whether to combat recession or control inflation. For Bitcoin, the emission is scheduled from the moment the network goes online.

- Pressure on gold reserves and energy consumption for Bitcoin: The limited increase in gold reserves has compromised the ability of the USA to increase the supply of dollars in circulation while maintaining its parity with gold. To some extent, concerns about the energy consumption required to secure the Bitcoin network may represent a threat to the network's long-term durability.

- Cost and inefficiency: Maintaining gold as a reserve requires storage and security costs. In addition, mining gold to support an expanding monetary base can be seen as an inefficient use of resources. As the Bitcoin network becomes more widely adopted, technical limitations will emerge, particularly in terms of transaction processing times and higher fees in the event of heavy use.

- Physical counterpart: While traditional fiat money does have physical notes and coins (or gold in the past with the gold standard), a large portion of it exists as digital data, similar to Bitcoin, which exists only in digital form and has no physical counterpart.

- Confidence: "Fiat" refers to money that a government has declared to be legal tender, but it is not backed by a physical commodity (gold-backed dollar until the early 1970s) but rather by the trust that individuals, and governments have that other parties will accept that currency. The value of both fiat money and Bitcoin is largely driven by trust and perception. Fiat money has value because people trust the government and the economic system. Similarly, Bitcoin holds value because its users have confidence in its technology and its scarcity.

- Stability: The value and stability of both fiat money and fiat-collateralized stablecoins are underpinned by trust in their issuing authorities. For fiat money, it is the trust in the government and central bank. For stablecoins, it is the trust in the issuing company's ability to maintain the peg to the fiat currency such as the

US dollar, Euro, or other national currencies. This means their value is directly tied to the value of the respective fiat currency, making them similar in terms of stability and valuation. Both can act as a store of value, such as gold, although the stability of stablecoins depends on the mechanisms maintaining their peg to fiat currencies.

Furthermore, the comparison of Bitcoin with monetarist and neoliberal reveals also several similarities.

One of the key concepts of monetarism is that the money supply should grow at a predetermined, slow, and stable rate, given that money does not affect real variables, but can affect inflation. Furthermore, monetarists consider that the central bank should give priority to restricting the quantity of money in circulation. These ideas are compatible with Bitcoin's code; new Bitcoins are created when a block is validated, the halving is programmed every 210,000 blocks, and the maximum quantity is 21 million Bitcoins.

Over the years, economic and monetary theory has played a key role in the way money is perceived and used. The twentieth century saw the development of several economic currents. Each of these movements took different approaches to economics and monetary policy in general and were more or less predominant at one time or another. However, the advent of digital technology has brought with it a new layer of complexity. The digital economy requires new methods of securing and authenticating transactions and data, which has become a major challenge in the information era. The cypherpunk movement, which emerged in the 1980s and 1990s, has its roots in the evolution of new technologies and their impact on privacy and individual freedom. As technological progress offered new perspectives, programmers, cryptographers, and activists came together to unleash the potential of cryptography to protect personal data. In 1976, a paper entitled "new directions in cryptography" addressed the concept of a distributed ledger was published. With advances in cryptography, another paper published under the title "Hot to Time-Stamp a Digital Document" in 1991 by Stuart Haber and Scott Stornetta introduced the concept of time-stamping the data rather than the medium.

Nevertheless, there are some incompatibilities regarding the origin and trust in currency. For Friedman, money gains its value from trust and credit in the monetary authority that issues it, whereas Bitcoin is not endorsed by any government or institution. Finally, monetarists do not preclude adjustments to monetary policy in response to economic conditions, which Bitcoin does not allow. By creating a decentralized, immutable, and self-sufficient system, Bitcoin is part of this movement centered on the defense of privacy and freedom in the digital age by offering the possibility of carrying out transactions without having to disclose one's identity and without possible censorship by third parties. Bitcoin could therefore be seen as a form of translation of crypto-anarchist ideas to economics and monetary policy.

The evolution of Bitcoin and other assets has helped to diversify and enrich the ecosystem while highlighting the importance of the "triangle of incompatibilities" that balances security, decentralization, and scalability. The Mundell-Fleming triangle, also known as the incompatibility triangle, is an economic theory developed by the monetarist economists Robert Mundell [7] and Marcus Fleming [8] in the 1960s. He conceptualized the limitations faced by countries seeking to pursue an independent economic policy in a globalized world.

VItalik Buterin applies the triangle of incompatibilities to the Blockchain, calling it the "Blockchain trilemma." Returning to the theoretical framework, he explains that a

Blockchain cannot fully satisfy all requirements and must choose between two of the following three objectives: the network's security is its ability to process transactions irreversibly, validating them to ensure their authenticity while effectively repelling attacks. This dimension guarantees that transactions, once recorded, cannot be altered or falsified. The second objective is decentralization, it reflects the idea that the network should not depend on a central authority or a single entity. By operating without a central body, it offers every participant uninterrupted and equal access to the network. The third and last objective taken into consideration in this trilemma is "scalability," representing the network's adaptability and responsiveness to increasing numbers of users and transaction volumes.

Buterin also identified some limitations inherent in Bitcoin's design. While recognizing Bitcoin's revolutionary advantages as a decentralized cryptocurrency, he found that its structure was unable to accommodate diversified applications and functions. For Buterin, this represented an obstacle to innovation in the sector. It was against this backdrop that he theorized the Blockchain trilemma. As a result, in 2013 Buterin began conceptualizing Ethereum, a platform that would incorporate full programmability without eliminating decentralization. Ethereum would be not just only a digital asset but also a platform for decentralizing any type of service or application. This vision was the driving force behind Ethereum's development and laid the foundations for what would be the next major evolution in the cryptocurrency space. Published on January 23, 2014, on the Bitcointalk forum. The main aim of the Ethereum white paper is to offer an open platform where developers could create any decentralized application (dApps) with no need to build a new Blockchain for each application [9]. The central idea was that rather than having separate Blockchains for each application (such as Bitcoin for peer-to-peer transfer or Namecoin for domain name resolution), there could be one universal platform for all kinds of applications. At the core of this vision was the introduction of "smart contracts," self-executing scripts that work when certain conditions are met. Ethereum's networking capabilities, *via* the use of smart contracts, allowed the field of possibilities opened up by Bitcoin to be extended even further. So far, Bitcoin's relatively small size compared to the financial sector as a whole means that it is not directly designed to influence macroeconomic variables, but as an innovative payment system.

2. Blockchain and smart contracts: how they work and use cases

The potential applications of smart contracts could range from simple financial transactions to the management of complex supply chains and the creation of decentralized voting systems. Moreover, until now, there has not been any technological innovation that has more potential to advance the supply chain industry than Blockchain technology. In finance, smart contracts enable the creation of decentralized financial instruments such as loans, bonds, decentralized exchanges (DEX), and even derivatives. These innovations have made it possible to carry out financial transactions without the need for a trusted third party, thereby reducing costs and increasing efficiency. The main feature that distinguishes Blockchain from traditional databases is the combination of distribution, decentralization, and a consensus mechanism. If a business needs decentralized information, Blockchain is generally the solution because it is more efficient and less expensive than a traditional database. The business does not need to rely on intermediaries to register, track, and maintain the transaction data's integrity.

Furthermore, the Ethereum white paper refers to smart contracts as “"more complex applications (than Bitcoin) in which digital assets are directly controlled by a small amount of code that executes various rules.” In simple terms, a smart contract is a computer protocol for defining the terms of an agreement between two parties, verifying its execution, and implementing it automatically (without human intervention) after the terms of the agreement have been written directly into lines of code. These contracts are stored and replicated on the Blockchain, which in principle guarantees their immutability and transparency.

Over the last few years, companies of all sizes have identified and tested dozens of Blockchain use cases and applications to help address operational problems, improve processes, and reduce business costs. These potential applications range from end-to-end process visibility and real-time product traceability to data security and transaction reconciliation. While these potential benefits are quite promising, some hurdles remain that prevent Blockchain technology from seeing widespread adoption. One of these key challenges is the lack of knowledge and understanding of this technology by executives and professionals. The aim of this section is, therefore, to clarify the functions and potential of this technology in the business world.

2.1 Smart contracts: functioning and trust-building benefits for an ecosystem of market participants

As an emerging technology with great potential, Blockchain offers a programmable environment for smart contracts. With the advantages of Blockchain, smart contracts have been widely used in Blockchain. Smart contracts can not only change the existing business model but also bring a lot of convenience to public life in reality [10]. The concept of a “smart contract” was first introduced in 1995 by Nick Szabo, who defined it as follows: “a smart contract is a set of commitments defined in digital form, including the agreement that the participants in the contract can implement these commitments” [11]. Therefore, smart contract, which is characterized by high development efficiency, low maintenance cost, and high execution accuracy, is a perfect fit for Blockchain technology. Indeed, it can be said that smart contract is one of the major characteristics of Blockchain technology. Being the core technology of Blockchain, Blockchain smart contract has become increasingly popular in Blockchain projects with great influence, such as Ethereum and Hyperledger.

With the advent of Blockchain technology, the smart contract has been defined and become possible. A smart contract is an integrated programming contract that can be embedded into any Blockchain data, transaction, or asset to create a system that forms a system, market, or asset managed by the program. Smart contracts can be found in a wide range of sectors. They can provide innovative solutions not only in the financial sector but also in business management such as assets, supervision, contracts, and others in the social system.

Contracts, whether for leases, mortgages, property sales, loans, or services, have been around for a very long time. Their purpose is to bring two parties together and to enforce the rights of each party. However, when one of the parties fails to fulfill its obligations, the result is a dispute and a considerable loss of time and money. This is how smart contracts come into play and provide innovative solutions. A simple way to understand smart contracts is to think of them as “programmable money.”. While both parties in a traditional contract must perform their responsibilities, smart contracts self-execute predefined actions when certain conditions related to a particular transaction are met (**Figure 2**) [6].

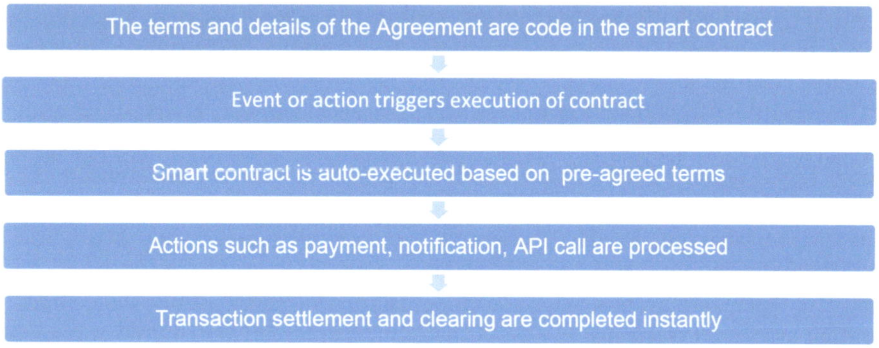

Figure 2.
Smart contract stages. Source: BusinessBlockchain.com.

The smart contract contains key data for both parties such as name, contact details, bank account details, and signatures, as well as information about the nature of the contract (lease, property sales, etc.), including the amount and payment date. When a smart contract is executed on the predefined payment date, it automatically withdraws the funds from the bank account and deposits them into the other party's account. This makes the procedure more systematic and organized and avoids any problems associated with late payment.

Following the progressive evolution of Blockchain technology, the development of smart contracts can be classified into three stages: Blockchain 1.0, 2.0, and 3.0 [10]. In Blockchain 1.0, the main application is Bitcoin. The contract is mostly used to realize cryptocurrency transactions, and its function is relatively limited. And RSK (rootstock), the smart contract development platform, which is based on the Bitcoin ecosystem, also needs to be strongly compatible with Ethereum at this stage [12].

In Blockchain 2.0, with the rise of smart contracts, DApp (decentralized application) can be built on Blockchain, which improves transaction speed. The system performance is also enhanced and presents diverse functions. Based on the openness of Blockchain, it can be divided into public Blockchain and consortium Blockchain [13]. Among these, the most common development platforms are Ethereum and Hyperledger Fabric in the public and consortium Blockchains, respectively. Finally, the Blockchain 3.0 is characterized by the development of the Blockchain ecology and the rise of new platforms [14] (i.e., side chain/cross chain, etc.) [15, 16] with the aim of providing solutions to the problems existing in Blockchain 2.0. At the same time, they are also highly anticipated and controversial. The most prominent platforms for the development of smart contracts are represented by Ethereum, Hyperledger Fabric, and EOS. As these three platforms continue to develop, we are able to understand how Blockchain technology, driven by smart contracts, can support the development of the real economy at a deeper level in a new form of cooperation.

Given the decentralized nature of Blockchain-based smart contracts and the nature of the contracts themselves, Blockchain-based smart contract applications can be separated into three technical categories: Ethereum, Hyperledger Fabric, and Enterprise Operation System (EOS).

The first one (Ethereum) is an open source and universal public Blockchain platform with the function of smart contracts, where the point-to-point contract is executed *via* its special cryptocurrency Ether (ETH) and Ethereum virtual machine

(EVM) [17]. Its applications cover sectors such as finance, smart grid, IoT, and sports quizzes. It can be used to create autonomous organizations, decentralized programs, and smart contracts.

The second, designed for use in the enterprise environment, is a modular and open-source licensed distributed ledger technology (DLT) platform for the corporate market. Key features include channel creation and pluggable implementation of multiple components [18]. It also offers innovation, adaptability, and optimization for insurance, banking, finance, real estate, healthcare, luxury, supply chain, and even digital music industries due to its modular and configurable architecture. An Enterprise Operation System (EOS) is a Blockchain underlying public Blockchain operating system. It is specifically developed for commercial distributed applications. It aims to achieve performance scalability of distributed applications by overcoming the issues of low performance, insufficient security, difficulty in development, and overdependence on transaction fees of existing Blockchain applications [19]. E-commerce, financial technology, and marketing are the main decentralized applications of EOS.

Moreover, the major difference between a smart contract and a traditional contract is that a smart contract uses computer language to record terms instead of legal language [20]. More precisely, smart contracts are automatically executed by a computing system and entirely stored in the computer. Smart contract built on Blockchain technology have the properties of tamper-proof and distributed transaction. Tamper proof is the main distinguishing characteristic of Blockchain, and its particular function is that once the smart contract has been successfully deployed, it can no longer be changed. Furthermore, thanks to the distributed function, each executed contract can be synchronized with each user's data terminal. In a smart contract, the contract terms are digitally deployed to the Blockchain network in code format and are automatically performed when the trigger terms of the protocol set are met. These features make smart contracts ideal for contract term scenarios as they can reduce malicious manipulation and human intervention [21]. The use of smart contracts is still developing, mainly in the financial and government sectors. Programmable currency and financial functions can be achieved through smart contracts. In addition, smart contracts can increase the degree and efficiency of automatic transactions, decrease the costs of transaction and execution, and simplify the control of transaction actions. Hence, it has caught the attention of financial organizations and central banks. In addition, smart contracts have broad application prospects such as cloud computing, financial assets, property sales, digital payment, IoT, and sharing economy [22]. The importance of Blockchain is characterized by the interconnection and cooperation of different parts, rather than a single part, allowing the smart contract to play a central role. This is to say that a large number of practical functions can be done on the Blockchain, and the current application system can achieve a level of transparency and trust that is unprecedented [23].

2.2 Smart contract applications: supply chain and donation examples

According to the latest report by PwC (Pricewaterhouse Coopers), 2025 will be a turning point if Blockchain is widely applied across the world. Moreover, by 2030, the application of Blockchain will lead to a growth of $1.76 trillion in global GDP (1.4% of global GDP) [24]. As a result, Blockchain can not only boost the development of technological innovation but also be a driving force for the world economy.

Countries around the world have developed the overall strategy for the development of the Blockchain industry, and Blockchain technology seems to have become the next playing field. Foreign giants, such as Google, Microsoft, JPMorgan Chase, Facebook, Amazon, and IBM, have all started to study Blockchain technology and introduced related technical solutions and applications. The Blockchain ecosystem embraces all aspects of the global economy and society. This technology has experienced exponential development and has been applied to areas such as intelligent manufacturing, financial services, tokenization of property, supply chain management, social welfare, and healthcare [25, 26].

In recent years, Blockchain technology has attracted the attention of central banks and financial institutions all over the world with smart contracts being the most significant characteristic of Blockchain applications. Thus, smart contracts can be applied to address fair trading or security problems in the financial sphere. In the Ethereum platform, to address the problem that the centralized TTP may expose the contract content, Zhang et al. [27] suggested a fair contract signing scheme for both parties using the Ethereum smart contract. In the signing process, the automatic smart contract is used to replace the original TTP agreement. This provides the fairness of signing to a certain extent, but the signature verification process cannot be performed directly by the smart contract. To address the problem that taxi charging is carried out by a third party, which causes conflicts between drivers and passengers, Zhang et al. [28] developed a secure charging protocol for agent driving service that is based on a Blockchain smart contract. Thus, the protocol removes the presence of an online third party *via* a publicly verified smart contract on the Blockchain of both parties, which ensures the fairness and transparency of the charging process. However, this agreement only applies to a "one-to-one" situation. Moreover, the use of smart contracts can be found also in the operations related to electronic cars. To tackle the problem that the charge indicated by an electric vehicle charging system may be different from the actual charge, and the potential security and privacy issues caused by the unreliable and opaque energy market, Sheikh et al. [29] proposed the consensus algorithm of energy security exchange. The goal is to process transactions on smart contracts, even if the processing cost is higher and the scalability needs to be improved. In the financial transaction sector, Ethereum has evident advantages in the public Blockchain. Besides being able to achieve procedurally secured transactions and financial contracts, in the public Blockchain, the synergy strength allows the contracts in Ethereum to fulfill different functions. As a result, this means that any application created on Ethereum can theoretically use the features of other applications. In addition, Hyperledger Fabric is more suitable for handling transactions on the consortium Blockchain. Since the official version was released, Fabric has been supported by many financial institutions, with many banks, using Fabric to create a consortium Blockchain, to realize Blockchain-based business innovation. Both technologies (Ethereum and Hyperledger Fabric) have their specific advantages, but the main point is to solve the problems of privacy and scalability.

Through smart contracts, all data in the supply chain can be displayed in real time. In addition, the decentralized, tamper-proof, and traceable nature of Blockchain facilitates inventory tracking at a detailed level, ensuring the security and reliability of all information in the supply chain and minimizing the risk of theft and fraud. In order to solve the problem of product information traceability in cross-border business of manufacturing companies, Xu et al. [30] designed a smart management scheme for manufacturing supply chain based on Ethereum Blockchain. It employs smart contract to implement process management and cross-chain architecture and ensures the compatibility, scalability, and security of the system. For the medical treatment of COVID-19, there were issues like inefficiency, one-point failure, and traceability in the existing system for handling the forward supply chain of COVID-19 medical equipment and the waste generated from medical equipment. To overcome these difficulties, AHMAD et al. [31] conceived and implemented the COVID-19 medical device supply chain based on Ethereum and IPFS (interplanetary file system) technologies. The purpose is to improve the data traceability of waste disposal and to implement automatic management by using intelligent contracts. Yet, data confidentiality and system scalability need to be promoted. Nirav et al. [32] presented an agricultural food supply chain system (KranTi) using Blockchain and a 5G network, which implements an automated credit payment system by using smart contracts. As a result, this technology is used to control the data flow of each role in the supply chain, as well as to manage order transactions and provide traceability of farmers' financial data and goods information, although the overall cost is relatively high. To support information sharing in supply chain inventory management, Tobias et al. [33] developed a decentralized information-sharing model using Fabric. It applies chain code to handle the transaction process and realizes the administration of complex multi-access rights. In addition, it can secure the implementation of privacy policy in the process of information sharing. However, it is not suitable for large-scale applications due to the low-performance benchmark and poor scalability. To summarize, Blockchain smart contract is mainly used to solve the problems of data transparency, information traceability, and supervision in the supply chain. Thus, it can greatly simplify the transaction process in practical application areas.

The management of humanitarian information is often hampered by unreliable information and information silos between different humanitarian actors. Frictions can cause the exchange of assets between two parties to be slow or hindered. Tax, regulation, bureaucracy, fraud, intermediary participation, etc. are just some of the reasons for friction that can lead to increased costs or deadlines. The distributed register of the Blockchain enables it to address these problems by sharing information across the network instead of being held by a single party. Members can validate transactions and verify the identity of each participant. All members of the network of the "permissioned" network also have a unique identity, as well as different roles and access rights to information. The network's secureness through cryptography and permissions significantly decreases the risk of unauthorized access to perform fraudulent acts. Also, with the consensus mechanism, all transactions are validated before being recorded in the Blockchain, which is inviolable and immutable. Supply chain visibility and data traceability can often be complex or impossible due to the dynamic nature of the humanitarian supply chain. Humanitarian operations can be significantly improved by increased supply chain transparency, which provides data to make decisions more efficiently and accurately and enables evidence-based interventions and management by exposing supply chain issues. This could lead to more effective treatment and increased accountability for different stakeholders. Blockchain offers the potential to increase transparency in the humanitarian supply chain. By providing a shared registry through a platform that enables the traceability and destination of physical humanitarian aid. This technology allows users to know who has handled different physical assets throughout the supply chain and how those assets have been transformed along the way. It allows for breaking down information silos by revealing the origin of a product from the supplier/donor to the final beneficiary. Thus, instead of waiting for reports at the end of a humanitarian mission, Blockchain can ensure a real-time record of all activities and products. This provides for closer collaboration, less duplication of resources, improved accountability, and more time efficiency. After applying Blockchain in the supply chain of the humanitarian sector, several studies highlight the added value of applying this technology in the financial supply chain of associations. Therefore, there is a real challenge to establish a peer-to-peer funding network to strengthen current funding models to reach people in need much faster and without the intermediation of a trusted third party, such as banks. This would cut the cost of financing international humanitarian aid. There is a need for more transparent, flexible, and efficient solutions for the organization of donations, as well as greater transparency and visibility of the use of these donations to reduce fraud and corruption, but also to identify funding gaps. Blockchain would, therefore, allow associations to better manage the distribution of donations and ensure that they are properly used to reach the final beneficiaries while having a record of each transaction that is distributed and publicly available.

3. Focus on the regulatory framework: a comparative study

It was during the period from 2014 to 2017 that institutional actors began to signal their interest in digital assets and in the opportunities offered by the Blockchain technology. The first traditional financial players to take an interest in Blockchain were venture capital funds. These investment funds quickly proved to be essential intermediaries between Silicon Valley's "traditional technology" sector financiers and the foundations/teams working on the development of Blockchain initiatives. They will also help to attract the interest of certain retail investors, whose options have been strengthened by the arrival of "smart money" in the crypto market. Although existing regulations to date are mainly national [34], some international organizations are taking a stand on the subject of digital asset regulation. In June 2014, the Financial Action Task Force, an organization set up to establish international standards to prevent money laundering and the financing of terrorism, took an interest in digital assets for the first time. In a report published in 2015 [35] and completed in 2019 [36] it suggested guidelines not for a ban but for a risk-based approach to digital assets, and to strengthen international cooperation for an effective regulation. In December 2022, the Bank for International Settlements published a report entitled "prudential treatment of crypto-asset exposures" [37] in which it announced that from January 2025, commercial banks would be able to hold 1% of their Tier 1 capital in crypto-assets, and up to 2% for their Tier 2 capital.

3.1 The European and North American legislation

In 2012, the European Central Bank (ECB) published its first report on virtual currencies. It acknowledged not only their existence but also highlighted the associated risks [38]. In 2014, the more conservative European Banking Authority (EBA) warned of the risks associated with virtual currencies, suggesting that banks should be discouraged from buying, selling, or holding them and that exchange platforms should be subject to the anti-money laundering directive [39]. In 2017, the European Securities and Markets Authority issued warnings about the risks associated with ICOs [40]. In 2018, the European Union adopted rules to regulate crypto-assets as part of the fifth Anti-Money Laundering Directive (AMLD5). In a statement made in 2019, Mario Draghi considers that Bitcoin and digital assets do not fall within the ECB's remit, and the does not classify them as money but as assets. In France, the regulation of crypto-assets is framed by articles 85 to 88 of the 2019 PACTE (Action Plan for Business Growth and Transformation) law [41], which establishes transparency and investor protection requirements for crypto-asset issuers. In compliance with European AML directives, supervision of digital asset service providers (DASPs) and issuers of token offerings to the public at the French Financial Markets Authority (AMF). Issuers of tokens must obtain an optional visa from the AMF to be able to communicate about the operation to French investors [42]. In September 2020, the European Commission published a proposal for a Markets in Crypto-Assets (MiCA) regulation aimed at harmonizing the regulation of digital assets within member states. After years of negotiations between European co-legislators, the MiCA regulation, based largely on the French model and reinforced by stricter requirements in terms of share capital, risk management, supervision, and control, was adopted on April 20, 2023. It is scheduled to come into force on January 1, 2025 [43].

Around 11% of Americans [44] and 13% of Canadians [45] will own digital assets in 2021. In North America, the regulation of digital assets in the U.S. and Canada share the common feature of being two federal states within which state regulation is important. However, the approaches of U.S. and Canadian regulators differ in several respects. It is hard to find uniformity in the legal treatment of digital assets in the U.S. among the various federal agencies. The Financial Crimes Enforcement Network (FinCEN) does not consider cryptocurrencies to be legal tender, but since 2013 it has considered exchanges to be money transmissions (under its jurisdiction) and considers tokens to be "other value that substitutes for money." The Security Exchange Commission defines a security as a financial instrument issued by individuals, corporations, and governments that is traded on a financial market [46]. The SEC generally considers that "coins," such as Bitcoin, are not securities because they do not represent an ownership or profit interest in a company, and they function as a "form of currency and are used to conduct transactions on a decentralized network [47]". Tokens, on the other hand, can take a variety of forms and may be considered securities by the SEC depending on their nature and use. If a token meets the definition of a security, it is subject to securities regulation and must be registered with the SEC unless it meets an exemption. From a tax perspective, the internal revenue service (IRS) considers digital assets to be property and taxes them as such. The coins or tokens obtained from mining are taxed as gross income at the value of the digital asset on the day it is obtained.

On June 19, 2014, Canada enacted Bill C-31, the world's first federal crypto-asset legislation, subjecting "virtual currencies" to the same obligations as money services businesses regulated under anti-money laundering laws. However, Ontario, home to the country's largest capital markets, is making its own decisions on access, although it is looking to the primary regulator for guidance. The CSA, in conjunction with IIROC (the Investment Industry Regulatory Organization of Canada, the regulatory umbrella for the provincial regulators), has published clear guidelines for crypto-asset companies, emphasizing that public dialog is encouraged and that these guidelines are not permanent, but will evolve with the cryptocurrency world.

3.2 Regulation in Bresil, Argentina, Japan and China

In February 2014, the Banco Central do Brasil (BACEN) warned the Brazilian public about the use of crypto-assets [48] and specifically highlighted their volatility. This instability was attributed to various factors, such as the low volume of transactions and the lack of recognition of crypto-assets as a reliable payment instrument. Although BACEN was aware of these risks, it did not introduce strict regulations at the time, leaving itself open to intervene later in the situation. The Federal Revenue Service (Receita Federal) has established guidelines for the declaration of crypto-assets. In fact, already at the end of 2014, it required that Bitcoins be declared under the category of "other goods and rights." Thus, Bitcoins were considered similar to financial assets and were defined as "income" received in the form of goods or rights valued in currency. Consequently, if a Bitcoin transaction generates a profit of more than R$35,000, this profit is subject to a 15% tax.

Crypto-assets are an innovation that does not easily coexist with the current legal Argentinian structure (Ley 26.831 de Mercado de Capitales) and requires legal adaptations. The Central Bank of the Argentine Republic (BCRA) has warned of the risks associated with crypto-assets and has declared its competence to regulate them, but has not yet established concrete regulations. The Financial Information Unit (UIF), responsible for the prevention of money laundering, has recognized crypto-assets and has established the need for increased monitoring of transactions involving these currencies [49]. In 2019, the BCRA implemented restrictions to prevent currency outflows when trading crypto-assets, but foreign exchange firms in Argentina said they could still acquire crypto-assets with Argentine pesos. The country, still affected by hyperinflation (+113.4% year-on-year in July 2023), wants to prevent a drain on the country's dollar reserves, while an increasing number of Argentines see Bitcoin and stablecoins as an alternative to the current monetary system and a means of protecting their purchasing power against inflation [50].

In April 2017, Japan recognized Bitcoin as legal property under the Payment Services Act. The Virtual Currency Act of 2017 [51] allows cryptocurrencies to be used to make payments. The regulatory framework regulates exchanges. Exchanges must comply with anti-money laundering and anti-terrorist financing obligations. Foreign platforms are also allowed to offer their services in Japan as long as they are subject to similar obligations. Completely anonymous digital assets are strictly forbidden. Japan's originality is symbolized by the Japan Virtual Currency Exchange Association (JVCEA). The JVCEA was established in October 2018 by 16 digital asset exchanges operating in Japan. JVCEA is a self-regulated organization recognized by the FSA. The association is working on various issues, such as the integrity of exchanges and the amount of customer assets held in hot wallets, which are more susceptible to theft. The offering of digital assets to investors is under the supervision of the FSA, which is responsible for the approval of each listing. For example, USDT, the world's most traded digital asset, is not approved by the regulator, which considers the issuer to be risky. Regarding taxation, Japan has abolished value-added tax on exchanging cryptos for fiat currencies.

China banned crypto-assets and related activities (including mining and ICOs) in 2017 [52]. However, the use of Blockchain technology is not completely closed in China. In September 2018, the Hainan Free Trade Zone Blockchain Experimental District, where the Huobi exchange is headquartered, was approved by the Chinese Government. Additionally, China's central bank is the world's first to offer its own digital version of central bank money. This Central Bank Digital Currency (CBDC) is based on Blockchain, although the lack of decentralization of the network makes this technology almost "unnatural." Another example is Hong Kong, which is actively participating in the development of the Blockchain industry as its special status means that regulations are more favorable to digital assets.

The Russian Government has long been critical of digital assets [53]. In July 2020, the Russian Government adopted the Federal Law on Assets to Digital Financial Assets and Digital Currency, which sets out general concepts for the regulation of digital assets. According to a study by the United Nations Conference on Trade and Development (UNCTAD), despite a very theoretical framework for the sector, in 2022, Russia is the second country with the highest proportion of its population holding digital assets, after Ukraine (11.9 and 12.7%, respectively). In 2022, Kozhedubova and Kovaleva's study shows that by the end of 2020, Russia will be the country with the highest volume of undeclared digital asset transactions (41% of global transactions) and whose population will be the most targeted by cyberattacks involving crypto-assets (11.2% of global attacks).

4. Conclusion

In conclusion, the emergence of Blockchain and Bitcoin has significantly reshaped industries, providing innovative solutions to financial challenges and technological advancements. Satoshi Nakamoto's pioneering paper on Bitcoin established a decentralized, transparent ledger that addressed the critical issue of double spending. The evolution of this technology has led to the emergence of various cryptocurrencies and concepts, such as Ethereum's smart contracts and decentralized applications, which are transforming the crypto-asset landscape. Moreover, the Blockchain trilemma, which reflects the trade-off between security, decentralization, and scalability, is evident in the evolution of Bitcoin and the subsequent development of Ethereum. Ethereum's introduction of smart contracts addresses the limitations of Bitcoin's design and fosters a new era of decentralized applications. The programmable nature of the smart contract is revolutionizing various industries, particularly in finance and supply chain management.

Smart contracts, which operate on Blockchain platforms, such as Ethereum and Hyperledger Fabric, offer benefits such as increased efficiency, reduced costs, and greater transparency. Potential applications range from financial instruments to supply chain management, with real-world examples demonstrating the technology's transformative impact. As countries and businesses around the world recognize Blockchain's potential, overcoming challenges, such as understanding the technology, will be critical to widespread adoption. Blockchain's decentralized, tamper-proof nature is particularly relevant in supply chain management, ensuring real-time visibility and traceability. Applications in humanitarian efforts further demonstrate the potential for transparency, accountability, and efficiency. While challenges such as scalability remain, Blockchain's ability to reshape industries and redefine trust in transactions positions it as a critical technological innovation with far-reaching implications for the global economy.

There has been a notable shift in the regulatory landscape surrounding digital assets and Blockchain technology over the period studied from 2014 to 2023. The involvement of institutional actors, in particular venture capital funds, has played a crucial role in bridging the gap between traditional financial institutions and Blockchain initiatives. International organizations, such as the Financial Action Task Force and the Bank for International Settlements, have shown interest in establishing guidelines for a risk-based approach to digital assets, although existing regulations remain predominantly national. Overall, the regulatory landscape is evolving globally. Jurisdictions are shaping their approaches based on the unique challenges and opportunities presented by digital assets and Blockchain technology. To ensure effective and harmonized regulation in this rapidly evolving area, the adoption of international standards and cooperation will become increasingly important.

To conclude, this study provides an overview of the existence and implementation of Blockchain technology in the world's modern economy. It focuses on the ongoing development of smart contracts. It also takes a "theoretical" look at the characteristics of Blockchain, drawing on various economic theories and comparing common and different approaches. Given the importance of this technology, the functioning of the Blockchain and the mechanisms of smart contracts are presented. This has led us to present an overview of the use of Blockchain and smart contracts. Three main sectors have been analyzed: finance, supply chain, humanitarian donations, and supply chain. Given the importance of this new technology, the regulatory response of the world's economies is different. In this context, we present the main regulatory features of the EU, North America (USA and Canada), Japan, Brazil, Argentina, China, and Russia.

Author details

Jérôme Verny[1*], Yacine Aiat[2], Stephane Fourneaux[1] and Eric Lambourdière[3]

1 NEOMA Business School, Paris, France

2 HIGHFI – HF-LAB, Paris, Paris, France

3 Institute of Technology, University of French West Indies, Martinique, France

*Address all correspondence to: jerome.verny@neoma-bs.fr

References

[1] Bocek TM, Rodrigues BB, Strasser T, Stiller B. Blockchains everywhere - a use-case of Blockchains in the pharma supply-chain. 2017 IFIP/IEEE Symposium on Integrated Network and Service Management (IM). 2017:772-777. Available from: https://www.semanticscholar.org/paper/Blockchains-everywhere-a-use-case-of-blockchains-in-Bocek-Rodrigues/0356360ce4e31a901f5cc48b090af30f56bb3f2d

[2] Pann X, Song M, Ai B, Ming Y. Blockchain technology and enterprise operational capabilities: An empirical. International Journal of Information Management. 2020;**52**:101946

[3] Nakamoto S. Bitcoin: A Peer-to-Peer Electronic Cash System. 2008. Available from: https://Bitcoin.org/Bitcoin.pdf

[4] Shekhar SS. Understanding Blockchain technology. Computer Science and Engineering. 2018;**8**(2):23-29. DOI: 10.5923/j.computer.20180802.02

[5] Lambourdiere E, Corbin E, Verny J. Blockchain technology to address interoperable seafood traceability issues: A case study. In: 3rd Edition of the International Conference PROLOG. La Rochelle (France): HAL Open Science; 2017. Available from: https://hal.science/hal-04021600/

[6] Babich V, Hilary G. Distributed Ledgers and Operations: What Operations Researchers Should Know About Blockchain Technology. Forthcoming in Manufacturing & Service Operations Management, Georgetown McDonough School of Business Research Paper No. 3131250, (August 27, 2018). Available from: https://ssrn.com/abstract=3131250 or http://dx.doi.org/10.2139/ssrn.3131250

[7] Mundell RA. Capital mobility and stabilization policy under fixed and flexible exchange rates. The Canadian Journal of Economics and Political Science. 1963;**29**(4):475-485

[8] Fleming JM. Domestic financial policies under fixed and under floating exchange rates. IMF Staff Papers. 1962;**9**(3):369-380

[9] Ethereum White Paper. 2014. Available from: https://Ethereum.org/en/whitepaper

[10] Lin SY, Zhang L, Li J, et al. A survey of application research based on Blockchain smart contract. Wireless Networks. 2022;**28**:635-690. DOI: 10.1007/s11276-021-02874-x

[11] Nakamoto S. Bitcoin: A Peer-to-Peer Electronic Cash System. 2008. Available from: http://www.Bitcoin.org/Bitcoin.pdf

[12] Worley C, Skjellum A. Blockchain tradeoffs and challenges for current and emerging applications: Generalization, fragmentation, sidechains, and scalability. In: 2018 IEEE International Conference on Internet of Things (iThings) and IEEE Green Computing and Communications (GreenCom) and IEEE Cyber, Physical and Social Computing (CPSCom) and IEEE Smart Data (SmartData). 2018. pp. 1582-1587. Available from: https://ieeexplore.ieee.org/document/8726513

[13] Nofer M, Gomber P, Hinz O, Schiereck D. Blockchain, business & information. Systems Engineering. 2017;**59**(3):183-187

[14] Singh A, Click K, Parizi RM, Zhang Q, Dehghantanha A, Choo KKR.

Sidechain technologies in Blockchain networks: An examination and state-of-the-art review. Journal of Network and Computer Applications. 2020;**149**:102471

[15] Kannengießer N, Pfister M, Greulich M, Lins S, Sunyaev A. Bridges between islands: Cross-chain technology for distributed ledger technology. In: Hawaii International Conference on System Sciences 2020. Proceedings of the 53rd Hawaii International Conference on System Sciences, Available at SSRN: Maui, Hawaii, January 7-10, 2020. Available from: https://ssrn.com/abstract=3452714

[16] Deng L, Chen H, Zeng J, Zhang LJ. Research on cross-chain technology based on sidechain and hash-locking. In: Liu S, Tekinerdogan B, Aoyama M, Zhang LJ, editors. Springer, Cham: International Conference on Edge Computing. 2018;**10973**:144-151. DOI: 10.1007/978-3-319-94340-4_12

[17] Zhu LJ. New trend in Blockchain: From Ethereum ecosystem to enterprise applications. In: Proceedings of the 4th Global Conference of Knowledge Economy. Qingdao, Shandong Province, China: GCKE; 2017. p. 1 1

[18] Shi WB. The Blockchain System Based Hyperledger Fabric as Cloud Service. Hangzhou: Zhejiang University; 2018

[19] Luo X. Research and Implementation of Security Development and Debugging Platform for Smart Contract. Chengdu: University of Electronic Science and Technology of China; 2020

[20] Northern Trust Corporation. Northern trust marks a breakthrough in securities servicing by deploying legal clauses as smart contracts on Blockchain. Journal of Engineering. 2019. Available from: https://www.businesswire.com/news/home/20190415005220/en/Northern-Trust-Marks-Breakthrough-Securities-Servicing-Deploying.html

[21] Governatori G, Idelberger F, Milosevic Z, Riveret R, Sartor G, Xu X. On legal contracts, imperative and declarative smart contracts, and Blockchain systems. Artificial Intelligence Law. 2018;**26**(4):377-409

[22] He HW, Yang A, Chen ZH. Survey of smart contract technology and application based on Blockchain. Journal of Computer Research and Development. 2018;**55**(11):112-126

[23] Ba SS. The current situation and trend of the development of financial science and technology in China. Tsinghua Financial Review. 2017

[24] Northern Trust Corporation. Northern trust strengthens private equity audit via Blockchain technology with PwC. Journal of Engineering. 2018. Available from: https://www.businesswire.com/news/home/20180319005240/en/Northern-Trust-Strengthens-Private-Equity-Audit-Blockchain

[25] Yli-Huumo J, Ko D, Choi S, Park S, Smolander K. Where is current research on Blockchain technology? A systematic review. PLoS ONE. 2016;**11**(10):0163477

[26] Cao B, Lin L, Li Y, Liu YX, Xiong W, Gao F. Review of Blockchain research. Journal of Chongqing University of Posts and Telecommunications (Natural Science Edition). 2020;**32**(01):1-14

[27] Zhang L, Zhang H, Yu J, Xian H. Blockchain-based two-party fair contract signing scheme. Information Sciences. 2020;**535**:142-155

[28] Hang H, Deng E, Zhu H, Cao Z. Smart contract for secure billing in

ride-hailing service via Blockchain. Peer-to-Peer Networking and Applications. 2019;**12**(1):1346-1357

[29] Asfia U, Kamuni V, Sheikh A, Wagh S, Patel D. Energy trading of electric vehicles using Blockchain and smart contracts. In: Proceedings of the 18th European Control Conference (ECC). Institute of Electrical and Electronics Engineers (IEEE): Piscataway; 2019. pp. 3958-3963. Available from: https://ieeexplore.ieee.org/document/8796284

[30] Xu ZJ, Zhang J, Song ZX, Liu YC, Li J, Zhou JH. A scheme for intelligent Blockchain-based manufacturing industry supply chain management. Computing. 2021;**11**(1):1-20. DOI: 10.1007/s00607-020-00880-z

[31] Ahmad RW, Salah K, Jayaraman R, Yaqoob I, Ellahham S. Blockchain-based forward supply chain and waste management for COVID-19 medical equipment and supplies. IEEE Access. 2021;**9**(9):44905-44927

[32] Patel N, Shukla A, Tanwar S, Singh D. KRanTi: Blockchain-based farmer's credit scheme for agriculture-food supply chain. Transactions on Emerging Telecommunications Technologies. 2021. DOI: 10.1002/ett.4286. Available from: https://onlinelibrary.wiley.com/doi/abs/10.1002/ett.4286

[33] Guggenberger T, Schweizer A, Urbach N. Improving inter-organizational information sharing for vendor managed inventory: Towards a decentralized information hub using Blockchain technology. IEEE Transactions on Engineering Management. 2020;**67**(4):1074-1085

[34] Zeng SQ, Huo R, Huang T, Liu J, Wang S, Feng W. Survey of Blockchain: Principle, progress and application. Journal on Communications. 2020;**41**(01):134-131

[35] FATF. Guidance for a Risk-Based Approach. FATF/OECD: GAFI; 2015

[36] FATF. Guidelines for the Risk-Based Approach Applied to Virtual Assets and Service Providers Related to Virtual Assets. FATF: FATF; 2019

[37] FATF. Prudential Treatment of Cryptoasset Exposures. Banque des règlements internationaux. FATF; 2022

[38] Bank for International Settlements. Virtual Currency Schemes. BCE, Banque centrale européenne. Bank for International Settlements; 2012

[39] European Banking Authority EBA Opinion on 'virtual currencies'. Autorité Bancaire Européenne. European Banking Authority; 2014

[40] ESMA highlights ICO risks for investors and firms. Autorité Européenne des Marchés Financiers. ESMA highlights ICO risks for investors and firms; 2017

[41] LOI n° 2019-486 du 22 mai 2019 relative à la croissance et la transformation des entreprises (JORF n°0119 du 23 mai 2019)

[42] Alice BM, Faustine F, Alexandre L, William O'R, Claire P. Droit des crypto-actifs et de la Blockchain, Alice Barbet-Massin, Faustine Fleuret, Alexandre Lourimi, William O'Rorke, Claire Pion. LexisNexis; 2020

[43] Conseil européen. Finance numérique: le Conseil adopte de nouvelles règles sur les marchés de crypto-actifs. Conseil européen: Conseil européen; 2023

[44] Economic Well-Being of U.S. Households in 2021. Federal Reserve Board Publication; 2022

[45] Daniela B, Walter E, Christopher H, Kim H, Marcel V. Bank of Canada. Private Digital Cryptoassets as Investment? Bitcoin Ownership and Use in Canada. Bank of Canada; 2022

[46] Application of FinCEN's Regulations to Persons Administering, Exchanging, or Using Virtual Currencies. FIN-2013-G001. 2013

[47] Dans le cadre de la faillite de Celsius, le tribunal a autorisé l'entreprise à vendre ses Altcoins contre du Bitcoin pour se conformer aux exigences de la SEC. Available from: https://www.coindesk.com/policy/2023/06/30/bankrupt-celsius-can-convert-altcoins-to-btc-eth-starting-july-1-following-sec-talks/#:~:text=Celsius%20%E2%80%9Cmay%20sell%20or%20convert,2023%2C%E2%80%9D%20Glenn's%20ruling%20said

[48] Mendes AL, Feltrim LE. Banco Central do Brasil, Comunicado n° 25.306, de 19 de fevereiro de 2014. Available from: https://www.bcb.gov.br/estabilidadefinanceira/exibenormativo?tipo=comunicado&numero=25306

[49] Banco Central de la Republica Argentina. BCRA and CNV Warn about Risks and Implications of Crypto Assets. Banco Central de la Republica Argentina; 2021. Available from: https://www.bcra.gob.ar/noticias/alerta-sobre-riesgos-implicancias-criptoactivos-i.asp

[50] Chainalysis. Latin America's Key Crypto Adoption Drivers: Storing Value, Sending Remittances, and Seeking Alpha. Chainalysis Report; 2022

[51] Sonksen C. Cryptocurrency regulations in ASEAN, East Asia, & America: To regulate or not to regulate. Washington University Global Studies Law Review. 2021;**20**(1):171-199

[52] Public Notice of the PBC, CAC, MIIT, SAIC, CBRC, CSRC and CIRC on Preventing Risks of Fundraising through Coin Offering. Available from: http://www.pbc.gov.cn/en/3688110/3688181/3712144/index.html

[53] Gorchakova TE. On the Development of Crypto Industry of Japan. Восточная Азия: Факты и Аналитика; 2022

Chapter 3

Novel Cryptocurrency Investment Approaches: Risk Reduction and Diversification through Index Based Strategies

Stanislaw P. Stawicki

Abstract

Cryptocurrency investment approaches continue to evolve rapidly. Traditionally, cryptocurrency holders tend to actively support up to several distinct projects, focusing their selection criteria on specific project characteristics, project team and community, existing markets and liquidity levels, as well as the perception of each unique project's broadly understood "mission and vision" and "future potential." In this chapter, we will explore an index-based investment strategy as an alternative to the more traditional single- or oligo-asset approaches. In the index-based paradigm, multi-asset strategy involves equalization and redistribution of risk exposure across multiple, pre-vetted portfolio positions. This strategy, novel to the cryptocurrency space, also involves risk reduction through cost averaging, dilution of cyber security-related risk(s), as well as mitigation of liquidity restrictions related to individual-position market liquidity characteristics. Additional discussion of software platforms, including both custodial and non-custodial wallets, and the associated risk-benefit considerations, will also be included in this manuscript.

Keywords: cryptocurrency, diversification, index, investing, risk modulation

1. Introduction

Cryptocurrencies are among the most recent entrants into the "investment vehicle" arena, dating back to the late 2000's and the development and introduction of Bitcoin (BTC) as the first and prototypical cryptographically secured asset [1, 2]. Ever since the introduction of early cryptocurrencies, it became evident that these largely experimental assets are prone to significant manipulation and volatility, not to mention scamming and other forms of fraud [3, 4]. Consequently, research into the various safety-focused and financially optimized approaches to "cryptographic asset investing" (CAI) came to the fore of the contemporary investment community, driven largely by early adopters [5–7]. As interest in CAI grows among mainstream investors around the globe, many questions naturally arise among potential new market participants, with key concerns increasingly in-line with traditionally "mainstream"

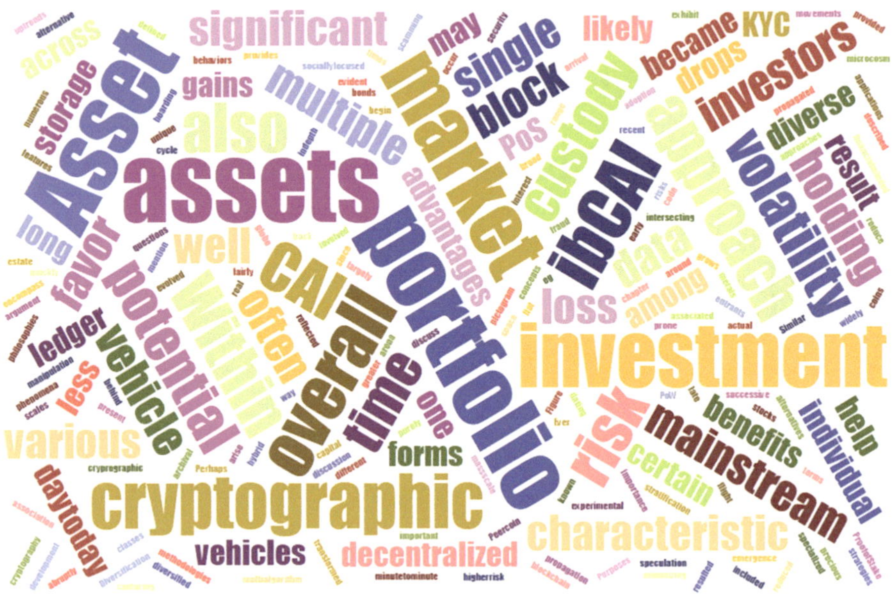

Figure 1.
A word cloud pictogram showing the high complexity of the overall cryptographic asset investment sphere. This asset space continues to evolve actively, with significant progress made since the 2010s, but a lot more work remaining to achieve full mainstream adoption.

issues (e.g., safekeeping, asset insurance, market liquidity and volatility, and other forms of guarantees) with each successive adoption cycle [8–10].

Among proposed strategies and approaches, index-based CAI emerged as one of the safest and less volatile options for long-term investors who are attracted by the potentially high returns associated with cryptographic assets, without the excessive exposure to risks associated with the traditionally high volatility of cryptocurrency markets [11–13]. In addition, index-based CAI (ibCAI) provides a degree of protection against any one component of the index itself becoming non-viable as an "investment vehicle," either due to hacking or other factors, such as a numerically dwindling cryptocurrency community or lack of project-specific infrastructure/support [14–17]. There are multiple intersecting concepts involved within the overall cryptographic investment space, reflected in **Figure 1** pictogram. This chapter will discuss the importance and potential advantages of ibCAI, with an in-depth discussion of risks, benefits, and alternatives associated with this approach. Other key concepts discussed herein will include ibCAI storage strategies, inclusive of various types of software platforms (e.g., wallets and multi-wallets) required for the successful implementation of individualized ibCAI portfolios.

2. Cryptocurrency basics: the "currency versus investment" argument

Initially intended to serve as alternative (and often idealized) media of exchange [18–21], cryptocurrencies fairly quickly evolved and transformed to encompass various philosophies and different methodologies of decentralized ledger propagation and verification. Purposes behind individual cryptocurrencies vary widely, from socially-focused platforms to specialized data archival instruments, to purely financial-minded applications [22–24]. Consequently, a broad range of phenomena and behaviors have been described in association with cryptocurrencies as "investment vehicles," from various forms of data storage to conduits for mass-scale speculation and hoarding [25, 26].

Diversification within the cryprographic asset "investment vehicle" microcosm can be defined across numerous stratification categories. Perhaps the most important characteristic of each unique cryptographic asset is the way the actual decentralized ledger is propagated, from block to block [27, 28]. While the early pioneers, such as Bitcoin and Litecoin belonged to the so-called Proof-of-Work (PoW) family of cryptocurrencies [29, 30], the arrival of Peercoin introduced Proof-of-Stake (PoS) as an alternative [31, 32]. Further code development resulted in "hybrid" PoW and PoS block verification [33]. Further, diverse cryptography approaches have also been employed in parallel, with the emergence of multi-algorithm coins that provided greater overall blockchain security [34, 35].

3. The argument "in favor of" index-based cryptographic asset investment approach

Similar to traditional financial markets and other mainstream "investment vehicles," cryptography-based assets exhibit certain characteristic (and at times predictable) features. In fact, analogous general approaches can apply to both individual cryptocurrencies and index-based vehicles alike. To begin with, ibCAI provides reduced minute-to-minute and day-to-day volatility [36]. Moreover, potential risk reduction benefits may also be present when cryptographic-based assets are included within a portfolio consisting of other asset classes (e.g., precious metals, commodities, real estate, fiat currencies, stocks, and bonds) [37, 38]. In the author's personal observations, the smoothing effect of multi-class asset portfolios can substantially reduce overall volatility, but at the same time is less likely to result in above-average gains (and losses) characteristic of higher-risk, less diversified strategies.

It has long been known that long-term investment portfolio gains correlate with minimizing downside losses during market drops [39, 40]. It is also well established that market drops occur more abruptly (both in terms of time scales and price movements) than most market uptrends [41, 42]. Perhaps less known fact about market drops is that the overall "universe of assets" must account for both gains and losses, and that efficient market operations result in risk-based concentration of wealth (e.g., those who make risky bets in volatile markets, stand to gain more than those who are risk averse) [43, 44]. Consequently, a highly diverse portfolio, complete with defensive assets and non-traditional assets, such as cryptocurrencies and commodities, may help reduce the overall "downside risk" by more effectively capturing the flight of capital during significant market upheavals [45–48]. One can also reason (at least for most investors) that in the long run, "fewer overall losses" strategy will tend to outperform various "high gain / high loss" strategies, provided that the occasional "large losses" incurred in the latter are more likely to eclipse any "short-term gains" associated with high-risk bets.

Similar observations have been noted by our ibCAI expert group. More specifically, there are fairly well defined asset migration cycles between our large-cap, mid-cap, and small-cap portfolios. Such asset migration is highly reminiscent of stock market cycles based on indexed asset capitalization (small-, mid-, and large-caps) [49, 50]. For investors with shorter and medium-term horizons, this represents an excellent opportunity to "play the market" while reducing their overall downside risk. At the same time, those who own a balanced portfolio of assets across all market capitalization categories, are able to enjoy the "long and steady" rise of their entire portfolio, without the need to worry about day-to-day asset class fluctuations [51–53].

Finally, additional important arguments "in favor of" a more diversified ibCAI portfolio have to do with liquidity and cybersecurity considerations. In terms of market liquidity, it is well established that low-liquidity markets can be easily overwhelmed by large-scale buy or sell orders, resulting in heightened volatility and limited options for market entry / exit tactics [54, 55]. Given the often brutal realities of low-liquidity cryptocurrency markets, investors have coined the term "pump and dump" where timing of market entry/exit must be very precise, or one will end up "holding the bag" once the post-rally market liquidity dries up [56, 57]. Asset holders within a well-balanced ibCAI portfolio are therefore more likely to be able to exit markets (at any given time) without triggering significant market declines due to inherently low market liquidity.

In terms of cybersecurity-based considerations, a more diversified cryptocurrency portfolio provides significant protection against single-position or even few-positions loss due to hacking. Under such circumstances, the diversity of blockchains within an individual portfolio, along with the equal distribution of funds across all of the participating assets, reduces the overall single-position risk to (1/n) where "n" represents the total number of assets within the portfolio. In other words, a successful hack and a resultant loss of one of the positions in a portfolio of 30 positions will result in an overall loss of only 3.3%. This aspect of ibCAI portfolio management is often overlooked in favor of holding either a single or only a handful of assets.

4. Asset custody and reliability issues: know-your-customer (KYC) and other privacy related considerations

In the realm where privacy and confidentiality reign supreme, any approach to CAI is bound to meet the ever-present eyes of various regulatory agencies and entities responsible for taxation, legal and custody issues, and other aspects of financial market oversight [58–60]. For the purposes of this chapter, we will take a long-term view of traditional (non-speculative) investment approaches. In fact, the very concept of ibCAI represents the opposite of speculative, high-risk approaches of day-trading (e.g., time horizons of minutes to hours) and short-term (e.g., time horizons of <12 months) trading [61–63].

Inherent to the long-term stability and reliability of any "investment vehicle," whether traditional or non-traditional, is one's ability to reasonably closely follow the value and status of the portfolio/ holdings, as well as the general perception that the assets "will still be there" at the time of expected future redemption [64–66]. Thus, the issue of (legal) custody and associated systemic guarantees are central to such long-term stability. Moving further along this line of reasoning, the concept of "know-your-customer" (a.k.a., KYC) is also very important. After all, KYC-specific considerations (assuming that funds were initially procured in an honest/legitimate way) are among key protections the customer/holder has at his or her disposal to prove their ownership of a specific lot of cryptographic asset(s). In addition, KYC-based protections can also help prove that specific assets were lost to theft, even if investigations of said claim(s) are long and/or delayed [67–69].

5. Multi-wallets: the optimal individual investor approach?

Multi-wallet is a term that describes specialized software that is designed to securely hold multiple cryptocurrencies within a single shell or visual interface/container [70, 71]. Two broad categories of multi-wallets exist – Custodial and non-custodial. The former entails third-party control over end-user cryptocurrency private keys/account(s), with a well-defined set of vulnerabilities and potential downsides inherent to lack of direct end-user control [72, 73].

Non-custodial wallets, on the other hand, enable the end-user to fully control all aspects of the cryptographic asset custody and access considerations [74]. That said, there are important data security considerations, with significant vulnerabilities and opportunities for criminal exploitation of asset via both social engineering techniques and software hacking [70, 75]. Consequently, it is recommended at this time that individual users not only diversify their cryptocurrency portfolios, but also diversify the multi-wallets within which these portfolios are held.

With the introduction of simplified payment verification (SPV) methodology, transition from the more rigid architecture of "desktop-based wallets" (DBW) to "mobile-based multi-wallets" (MBMW) became possible [76, 77]. With the emergence of MBMWs, the end-user gained the power to essentially design his or her own, highly customized and personalized "do-it-yourself" (DIY) cryptocurrency portfolios. Such portfolios are complete with real-time price data inputs, user ability to determine and control asset ratios, as well as aggregate reporting of individual asset and portfolio values. Some software platforms, such as the Komodo Wallet, offer a multi-folio option, where several parallel portfolios can be created, each with its own set of private keys and secure password (**Figure 2**) [78, 79].

Figure 2.
An example of a software multi-wallet (Komodo Wallet) that constitutes a self-contained portfolio of cryptographic assets. Each asset is represented by its own line entry, complete with asset name, ticker symbol, current price, price change over a period of time, and other customized interface features.

Vaults and other multi-stakeholder custodial solutions have also been introduced, where assets are essentially "irretrievably locked" until a certain pre-defined number of authorized users "agree in principle" to release such assets to a third-party address [80]. This approach represents an attractive option for multi-person entities, such as families or small investment clubs, where assets can only be moved when a pre-determined number of participants all agree on a specific transfer operation. The multi-signature "vault storage" approach has also been popular among owners of various high-value cryptographic assets (such as non-fungible tokens or NFTs) [81, 82].

6. Technical aspects of index-based approaches

The overall diversification of the blockchain/cryptocurrency space resulted in significant diversification of customized code that allowed alternative cryptocurrencies (e.g., "AltCoins") to proliferate within the early (2009–2017) phases of the cryptographic asset era [83, 84]. In the context of asset holding, the logistics of diversification became formidable because of the requirement for cryptocurrency-specific "wallets" to be deployed for each unique asset. Two durable alternatives emerged to help solve this conundrum – the previously outlined implementations of SPV [77] and asset tokenization (AT) [85]. The latter, in general, relies on a primary blockchain (such as Ethereum or Quantum) to provide an "entry point" for different token-assigned value units (e.g., a single token represents a pre-defined item, a primary asset, or some other quantity, etc.) that is then uniquely identified under its own "contract address" (or essentially a "subaccount" that then holds secondary assets/tokens on the primary blockchain).

At this time, both custodial and non-custodial approaches to ibCAI management exist, both for different blockchains and for various unique tokens/tokenized assets. As outlined in previous sections, each of the approaches, along with some other associated nuances, may have a unique risk-benefit profile. Each end-user is encouraged to carefully consider all of the available options before proceeding. Factors that need to be taken into consideration include one's technical/computer/blockchain expertise, financial risk tolerance, the choice between active or passive management styles, the balance between privacy versus convenience, and the availability of specialized adjunctive financial products (such as "asset loss" insurance policies) [86, 87]. Finally, one must consider portfolio entry/exit points, such as either centralized or decentralized cryptocurrency exchanges. After all, most wallets only "hold assets" but are not able to facilitate active on/off-boarding of said assets. This aspect of ibCAI management also requires careful and comprehensive evaluation of risks, benefits, and alternatives by the end-user.

7. Conclusion

Cryptographic assets are here to stay, and so is cryptographic asset investing (CAI). Within this greater universe of asset management options, index-based CAI represents an emerging and increasingly popular option for volatility and risk reduction, with multiple potential advantages when compared to single- or oligo-asset CAI strategy. More specifically, the ibCAI approach minimizes the magnitude of any single-asset loss due to hacking or other exploits. It also helps facilitate portfolio off-loading in the setting of low-liquidity markets. Asset custody and software-based conduits for secure storage of cryptocurrencies and cryptocurrency portfolios continue to evolve, and represent a significant potential risk/attack surface. The area of ibCAI is likely to evolve and mature over the coming years, with emerging legal, KYC, and tax frameworks that will help introduce this approach to cryptocurrency investment into the mainstream.

Author details

Stanislaw P. Stawicki
EWMCI, LLC., Bethlehem, Pennsylvania, USA

*Address all correspondence to: stawicki_ace@yahoo.com

References

[1] Nakamoto S. Bitcoin: A peer-to-peer electronic cash system. Decentralized Business Review. 2008;**1**(1):1-9

[2] Stawicki SP. Introductory chapter: Early applications and evolution of Blockchain implementations in medicine. In: Blockchain in Healthcare: From Disruption to Integration. Cham, Switzerland: Springer; 2023. pp. 1-5

[3] Barnes P. Crypto currency and its susceptibility to speculative bubbles, manipulation, scams and fraud. Journal of Advanced Studies in Finance (JASF). 2018;**9**((18)):60-77

[4] Twomey D, Mann A. Fraud and manipulation within cryptocurrency markets. Corruption and Fraud in Financial Markets: Malpractice, Misconduct and Manipulation. 2020:205-249

[5] Petukhina A, Trimborn S, Härdle WK, Elendner H. Investing with Cryptocurrencies-evaluating their potential for portfolio allocation strategies. arXiv preprint arXiv:2009.04461. 9 Sep 2020

[6] Elendner H. F5: Optimised crypto-currency investment strategies. White paper, 2018. Available from: https://f5crypto.com/wp-content/uploads/2023/06/F5_Crypto_Index_Whitepaper-1.pdf

[7] Andrianto Y, Diputra Y. The effect of cryptocurrency on investment portfolio effectiveness. Journal of Finance and Accounting. 2017;**5**(6):229-238

[8] Spenkelink H. The Adoption Process of Cryptocurrencies-Identifying Factors That Influence the Adoption of Cryptocurrencies from a Multiple Stakeholder Perspective. Enschede, Netherlands: University of Twente; 2014;**1**:1-103

[9] Saiedi E, Broström A, Ruiz F. Global drivers of cryptocurrency infrastructure adoption. Small Business Economics. 2021;**57**:353-406

[10] Alzahrani S, Daim TU. Analysis of the cryptocurrency adoption decision: Literature review. In: 2019 Portland International Conference on Management of Engineering and Technology (PICMET). Portland, Oregon: IEEE; 2019;**1**:1-11

[11] Hu Y, Rachev ST, Fabozzi FJ. Modelling crypto asset price dynamics, optimal crypto portfolio, and crypto option valuation. 2019. arXiv preprint arXiv:1908.05419

[12] Trimborn S, Härdle WK. CRIX an index for cryptocurrencies. Journal of Empirical Finance. 2018;**49**:107-122

[13] EWMCI. East-West Magnate Cryptocurrency Investments. 2023 [cited 2023 November 30]. 2023 Available from: https://ewmci.info/

[14] Grobys K, Sapkota N. Predicting cryptocurrency defaults. Applied Economics. 2020;**52**(46):5060-5076

[15] Stylianou K et al. Cryptocurrency competition and market concentration in the presence of network effects. Ledger. 2021;**6**:81-101

[16] Howson P, de Vries A. Preying on the poor? Opportunities and challenges for tackling the social and environmental threats of cryptocurrencies for vulnerable and low-income communities.

Energy Research & Social Science. 2022;**84**:102394

[17] Trump BD et al. Cryptocurrency: Governance for what was meant to be ungovernable. Environment Systems and Decisions. 2018;**38**:426-430

[18] Brunton F. Digital Cash: The Unknown History of the Anarchists, Utopians, and Technologists Who Created Cryptocurrency. Princeton, New Jersey: Princeton University Press; 2020

[19] Shapiro M. Crypto-egalitarian life: Ideational and materialist approaches to Bitcoin. Social Analysis. 2022;**66**(3):62-82

[20] Petz M, Eskelinen T. The politics of money utopias: Methodological utopian explorations of the Banjar and the Neocracy. International Journal of Community Currency Research. 2022;**26**(1):1-21

[21] Jóhannsson J. Sharing Economy Platforms: A Path towards Progress or Inequality?; 2017

[22] Ba CT, Zignani M, Gaito S. The role of cryptocurrency in the dynamics of blockchain-based social networks: The case of Steemit. PLoS One. 2022;**17**(6):e0267612

[23] Shrivastava G, Le D-N, Sharma K. Cryptocurrencies and Blockchain Technology Applications. Hoboken, New Jersey: John Wiley & Sons; 2020

[24] Stawicki S. Blockchain in Healthcare: From Disruption to Integration. Vol. 10. Cham, Switzerland: Springer Nature; 2023

[25] Vejačka M. Basic aspects of cryptocurrencies. Journal of Economy, Business and Financing. 2014;**2**(2):75-83

[26] Pernice IGA, Almosova A, Elendner H. Cryptocurrency: Speculative asset and medium of exchange. 2021. SSRN 3964372. Available from: https://papers.ssrn.com/sol3/Delivery.cfm/SSRN_ID4069505_code3039903.pdf?abstractid=3964372&mirid=1

[27] Stawicki SP, Firstenberg MS, Papadimos TJ. What's New in Academic Medicine? Blockchain Technology in Health-Care: Bigger, Better, Fairer, Faster, and Leaner. Medknow; 2018. pp. 1-11

[28] Aggarwal S, Kumar N. Cryptographic consensus mechanisms. In: Advances in Computers. Philadelphia, Pennsylvania: Elsevier; 2021. pp. 211-226

[29] Auer R. Beyond the Doomsday Economics of 'Proof-of-Work' in Cryptocurrencies. Basel, Switzerland: Bank of International Settlements; 2019

[30] Capponi A, Olafsson S, Alsabah H. Proof-of-work cryptocurrencies: Does mining technology undermine decentralization? Management Science. 2023;**6**:1-53

[31] Bentov I, Gabizon A, Mizrahi A. Cryptocurrencies without proof of work. In: International Conference on Financial Cryptography and Data Security. Cham, Switzerland: Springer; 2016

[32] Zhao W et al. On peercoin proof of stake for blockchain consensus. In: 2021 The 3rd International Conference on Blockchain Technology. Kuala Lumpur, Malaysia. 2021;**3**:129-134

[33] Chepurnoy A. et al., Twinscoin: A cryptocurrency via proof-of-work and proof-of-stake. Cryptology ePrint Archive. 2017. Available from: https://eprint.iacr.org/2017/232.pdf

[34] Lovejoy JPT. An Empirical Analysis of Chain Reorganizations and Double-Spend Attacks on Proof-of-Work Cryptocurrencies. Boston, Massachusetts: Massachusetts Institute of Technology; 2020

[35] Arab Monetary Fund. Abu Dhabi, United Arab Emirates: Digital Currency Technologies; 2021;**23**:1-37

[36] Chabakauri G, Rytchkov O. Asset pricing with index investing. Journal of Financial Economics. 2021;**141**(1):195-216

[37] Čiumakovas I. Diversifying Your Portfolio with Cryptocurrency-Does it Improve Sharpe Ratios for Institutional Investors?. Enschede, Netherlands: University of Twente; 2022

[38] Rudolf KO, El Zein SA, Lansdowne NJ. Bitcoin as an investment and hedge alternative. A DCC MGARCH model analysis. Risks. 2021;**9**(9):154

[39] Jorion P. Risk management lessons from long-term capital management. European Financial Management. 2000;**6**(3):277-300

[40] Johansen A, Sornette D. Shocks, crashes and bubbles in financial markets. Brussels Economic Review. 2010;**53**(2):201-253

[41] Fama EF. The behavior of stock-market prices. The Journal of Business. 1965;**38**(1):34-105

[42] Bond FD. Stock Prices: Factors in their Rise and Fall, Illustrated with Charts. Vol. 6. New York, New York: Moody's Magazine Book Department; 1911

[43] Sauer RD. The economics of wagering markets. Journal of Economic Literature. 1998;**36**(4):2021-2064

[44] Fong W. The Lottery Mindset: Investors, Gambling and the Stock Market. Cham, Switzerland: Springer; 2014

[45] Hyung N, De Vries CG. Portfolio diversification effects of downside risk. Journal of Financial Econometrics. 2005;**3**(1):107-125

[46] Bhansali V, Holdom J. Diversifying diversification: Downside risk management with portfolios of insurance securities. The Journal of Portfolio Management. 2021;**47**(6):101-113

[47] Adamiec L, Cernauskas D. Optimal number of assets for reduction of market risk through diversification. International Journal of Economics, Business and Management Research. 2019;**3**:45-54

[48] Bouri E, Shahzad SJH, Roubaud D. Cryptocurrencies as hedges and safe-havens for US equity sectors. The Quarterly Review of Economics and Finance. 2020;**75**:294-307

[49] Copeland MM, Copeland TE. Market timing: Style and size rotation using the VIX. Financial Analysts Journal. 1999;**55**(2):73-81

[50] Lucas A, Van Dijk R, Kloek T. Stock selection, style rotation, and risk. Journal of Empirical Finance. 2002;**9**(1):1-34

[51] Senthilkumar A, Namboothiri A, Rajeev S. Does portfolio optimization favor sector or broad market investments? Journal of Public Affairs. 2022;**22**:e2752

[52] Gupta A, Subramanian RA. Harvesting Sector Beta through Broad Sector Indices. Paris, France: MSCI Index Research; 2013

[53] Bender J et al. Portfolio of risk premia: A new approach to

diversification. The Journal of Portfolio Management. 2010;**36**(2):17-25

[54] Baxter G, Cartlidge J. Flying by the seat of their pants: What can high frequency trading learn from aviation? In: Proceedings of the 3rd International Conference on Application and Theory of Automation in Command and Control Systems. Naples, Italy; 2013

[55] Clunie J. Predatory Trading and Crowded Exits: New Thinking on Market Volatility. Petersfield, Hampshire, UK: Harriman House Limited; 2010

[56] Xu J, Livshits B. The anatomy of a cryptocurrency {Pump-and-Dump} scheme. In: 28th USENIX Security Symposium (USENIX Security 19). Santa Clara, California, USA; 2019

[57] Dhawan A, Putniņš TJ. A new wolf in town? Pump-and-dump manipulation in cryptocurrency markets. Review of Finance. 2023;**27**(3):935-975

[58] Peláez-Repiso A, Sánchez-Núñez P, Calvente YG. Tax regulation on blockchain and cryptocurrency: The implications for open innovation. Journal of Open Innovation: Technology, Market, and Complexity. 2021;**7**(1):98

[59] Aziz A. Cryptocurrency: Evolution & legal dimension. International Journal of Business, Economics and Law. 2019;**18**(4):31-33

[60] Martinčević I et al. Accounting and tax regulation of cryptocurrencies. Interdisciplinary Description of Complex Systems: INDECS. 2022;**20**(5):640-661

[61] Jacobs BI, Levy KN, Starer D. Long/short equity investing. Journal of Portfolio Management. 1993;**20**(1):52

[62] Schoenmaker D, Schramade W. Investing for long-term value creation. Journal of Sustainable Finance & Investment. 2019;**9**(4):356-377

[63] van Loon RJ. Long-term investing and the frequency of investment decisions. The Journal of Portfolio Management. 2021;**47**(8):86-104

[64] Siegel JJ. Stocks for the Long Run: The Definitive Guide to Financial Market Returns & Long-Term Investment Strategies. New York, New York: McGraw-Hill Education; 2021

[65] Gorton G, Winton A. Financial intermediation. In: Handbook of the Economics of Finance. Philadelphia, Pennsylvania: Elsevier; 2003. pp. 431-552

[66] Gelpern A, Gerding EF. Inside safe assets. Yale Journal of Register. 2016;**33**:363

[67] Kuperberg M. Blockchain-based identity management: A survey from the enterprise and ecosystem perspective. IEEE Transactions on Engineering Management. 2019;**67**(4):1008-1027

[68] Tironsakkul T. et al. Probing the mystery of cryptocurrency theft: An investigation into methods for taint analysis. 2019. arXiv preprint arXiv:1906.05754

[69] Bischoping G. Prosecuting cryptocurrency theft with the defend trade secrets act of 2016. University of Law Review. 2018;**167**:239

[70] Shi C, Guan Y. Forensic analysis of android cryptocurrency wallet applications. In: IFIP International Conference on Digital Forensics. Cham, Switzerland: Springer; 2023

[71] Lan R. et al. Horizon: A gas-efficient, trustless bridge for cross-chain transactions. 2021. arXiv preprint arXiv:2101.06000

[72] Au A, et al. Care, Custody, & Control (CCC): Identification, Quantification, and Mitigation of Cryptocurrency Custodial Risk: Cryptocurrency and Cyber Risk: Market Analysis and Perspectives. New York; 2020

[73] Barbereau T, Bodó B. Beyond financial regulation of crypto-asset wallet software: In search of secondary liability. Computer Law & Security Review. 2023;**49**:105829

[74] Sans T, Liu Z, Oh K. A decentralized mnemonic backup system for non-custodial cryptocurrency wallets. In: International Symposium on Foundations and Practice of Security. Cham, Switzerland: Springer; 2022

[75] Kushnirenko SP, Kharatishvili AG. Cryptocurrencies turnover and forensic analysis of the mechanism of committing crimes. Kutafin Law Review. 2023;**9**(4):774-792

[76] Faridi A, Siddiqui F. Improving SPV-based cryptocurrency wallet. In: Cybernetics, Cognition and Machine Learning Applications: Proceedings of ICCCMLA 2019. Cham, Switzerland: Springer; 2020

[77] Biryukov A, Tikhomirov S. Security and privacy of mobile wallet users in Bitcoin, dash, Monero, and Zcash. Pervasive and Mobile Computing. 2019;**59**:101030

[78] Beutin N, Boran D. The Great Web 3.0 Glossary. Frankfurt am Main, Germany: Deutscher Fachverlag GmbH; 2023

[79] Kiechl P. Extension and Standardization of a Blockchain Interoperability API. Switzerland: Zürich; 2021

[80] Swambo J. et al. Custody protocols using bitcoin vaults. 2020. arXiv preprint arXiv:2005.11776

[81] Das D et al. Understanding security issues in the NFT ecosystem. In: Proceedings of the 2022 ACM SIGSAC Conference on Computer and Communications Security. Copenhagen, Denmark, EU; 2022

[82] Ruan X. Exploring Vulnerabilities and Anomalies in NFT Marketplaces. Guelph, Ontario, Canada: University of Guelph; 2022

[83] Ciaian P, Rajcaniova M. Virtual relationships: Short-and long-run evidence from BitCoin and altcoin markets. Journal of International Financial Markets, Institutions and Money. 2018;**52**:173-195

[84] Bousfield D. Crypto-coin hierarchies: Social contestation in blockchain networks. Global Networks. 2019;**19**(3):291-307

[85] Caldarelli G. Wrapping trust for interoperability: A preliminary study of wrapped tokens. Information. 2021;**13**(1):6

[86] Sun M. A breakthrough of digital assets security in crypto insurance: Cyber risk prediction models. Research and applications towards mathematics and computer. Science. 2023:54

[87] Zuckerman A. Insuring crypto: The birth of digital asset insurance. University of Illinois Journal of Law, Technology and Policy. 2021:75-119

Chapter 4

The Architecture of Blockchain Technology and Beyond

Artina Bedjeti Baftijari and Leonid Nakov

Abstract

Blockchain technology utilizes a decentralized and distributed ledger system (a list of all transactions across a peer-to-peer network) to securely record transactions across a network of computers. Using this technology, participants can transfer value across the Internet without the need for a central third party. Blockchain is the cornerstone of cryptocurrencies, offering a secure and transparent framework for recording transactions along with its unknowns and benefits. In the realm of digital currencies like Bitcoin, blockchain functions as a decentralized ledger, documenting every transaction across a distributed network. Its pivotal roles include decentralization, transparency, immutability, consensus mechanisms, security, and mining. Collectively, blockchain technology furnishes the infrastructure that empowers cryptocurrencies, enabling them to function as decentralized, secure, and trustless systems for the transfer of value. The fundamental principles of blockchain contribute to the robustness and dependability of cryptocurrencies in the digital landscape.

Keywords: blockchain, distributed ledger, decentralization, cryptocurrencies, bitcoin

1. Introduction

Blockchain, a contemporary buzzword, is an evolving technology with a firm foothold in commercial, financial, governmental, and academic domains. Its architectural features, such as decentralization, cryptocurrency, and consensus, are pivotal in ensuring security. Blockchain comprises validated transaction blocks, and its decentralized structure, free from a single point of failure, enhances safety. This chapter delves into blockchain architecture and security considerations, exploring decentralization, mining, consensus, smart contracts, and more. It serves as a launchpad for delving deeper into the multifaceted realm of blockchain technology [1].

In essence, blockchain refers to a distributed database system where data is organized into interconnected blocks forming a chain. The substantial attention garnered by this concept stems from its inventive utilization of established technologies in a novel manner. The power of blockchain technology is intricately linked to the emergence of digital currencies, notably Bitcoin. It's crucial to note that Bitcoin and blockchain are distinct entities. Drawing a parallel, Bitcoin is to blockchain what electronic mail (e-mail) is to the Internet – one represents the product, while the other is the underlying technology enabling its existence.

The introduction to this chapter on blockchain architecture and security concerns underscores the transformative power of blockchain as a technology with broad applications across diverse sectors. Let us dissect the key points highlighted earlier:

- *Decentralization:* Decentralization of Blockchain is a fundamental characteristic that sets it apart from traditional systems. Instead of relying on a central authority, data is distributed across a network of nodes.

- *Cryptocurrency:* Like Bitcoin and Ethereum cryptocurrencies, they are often associated with blockchain technology. They utilize blockchain for secure, transparent, and decentralized transactions.

- *Consensus:* The mechanism of consensus is crucial for validating and verifying transactions in a blockchain. Different blockchains may use various consensus algorithms, such as Proof of Work (PoW) or Proof of Stake (PoS), to achieve agreement among nodes.

- *Security:* The security of blockchain stems from its inherent decentralization. By eliminating a single point of failure, it gains resilience against attacks. Every block is intricately linked to the preceding one through cryptographic hashes, establishing an immutable chain.

- *Cost-cutting:* Blockchain can lead to cost reductions by eliminating intermediaries, streamlining processes, and reducing the need for manual verification. Smart contracts, self-executing contracts with terms directly written into code, automate many processes.

- *Smart contracts:* Smart contracts are self-executing contracts with the terms directly written into code. They automate and enforce the terms of an agreement, reducing the need for intermediaries and increasing efficiency.

- *Mining:* Mining is the process by which new transactions are added to the blockchain. In PoW-based blockchains, miners solve complex mathematical problems to validate transactions and create new blocks.

- *Security concerns:* While blockchain is considered secure, there are still concerns such as potential vulnerabilities in the implementation of smart contracts, the 51% attack in PoW systems, and regulatory challenges.

Blockchain technology, as of the last quarter of 2023, is reshaping industries and fueling a new era. The increasing interest in blockchain and digital finances is evident across both private and public sectors, with governments globally supporting and adopting this transformative technology. Blockchain's crucial role in enhancing transparency and security has become indispensable, addressing critical concerns across various sectors. It is important to note that the blockchain space is dynamic, and developments may occur very fast. Here is a recap of the latest trends [2]:

- *DeFi (Decentralized finance):* The continued rise of decentralized financial applications providing services like lending and trading without traditional intermediaries.

- *NFTs (Non-fungible tokens):* The surge in popularity of NFTs, representing unique digital assets and fostering innovation in digital art, collectibles, and virtual real estate.

- *Interoperability:* Projects aiming to enhance interoperability between different blockchains, fostering a more connected and collaborative blockchain ecosystem.

- *Blockchain and AI integration:* Exploration of the integration of blockchain and artificial intelligence to leverage transparency for AI model accountability and secure data sharing.

- *Sustainability and green blockchain:* Increased awareness of the environmental impact of blockchain, leading to a focus on sustainable and eco-friendly alternatives, especially in the context of Proof of Work consensus mechanisms.

- *CBDCs (central bank digital currencies):* Various countries exploring or piloting their central bank digital currencies, using blockchain for more efficient and transparent financial systems.

- *Layer 2 solutions:* Efforts to address scalability concerns in blockchain networks through the development and adoption of Layer 2 solutions, including sidechains and off-chain scaling.

- *Privacy solutions:* Attention to enhancing privacy features on public blockchains and the development of privacy-focused blockchains to address concerns related to data confidentiality.

- *Blockchain in supply chain:* Increased adoption of blockchain in supply chain management for improved transparency, traceability, and efficiency in tracking the movement of goods.

- *Cross-industry blockchain adoption:* Expansion of blockchain technology beyond finance, finding applications in healthcare, real estate, logistics, and various other industries.

2. A look at blockchain technology: how does it work?

What is blockchain and why is so innovative?

The blockchain functions as a decentralized ledger, capturing a comprehensive record of all transactions within a peer-to-peer network. Through this technology, participants have the ability to exchange value over the Internet, bypassing the requirement for a central third party. Its innovativeness effectively tackled a long-standing challenge in the digital domain known as double spending [3], resolving an issue that had persisted for an extended period. Let us consider a simple case:

Dori and Aris are friends. Dori has $100 in her wallet, and Aris has none. Dori decides to transfer $100 to Aris. In the physical world, it's a straightforward exchange: Dori now has no money, and Aris has $100.

Simple, right?! But let us imagine the following situation:

In the digital scenario, Dori's transfer of a photo representing $100 to Aris introduces a unique challenge. Unlike the physical transfer of money, the digital photo is duplicable, leading to questions about its ownership and potential misuse. Did Dori retain a copy of the photo, share it with additional friends, or even post it publicly on social media where it could be freely downloaded? The inherent replicability of digital assets like these challenges the traditional notion of ownership and transfer, highlighting the need for a secure and trustworthy system to manage digital transactions. Blockchain technology, with its decentralized and tamper-resistant characteristics, aims to address such issues in the digital realm.

Digital Ledger

To address the questions raised earlier, we rely on the concept of a digital ledger. The key is to have a record of the quantity of $100 digital photos owned by Dori and how she distributes them among her friends. However, it's not Dori's responsibility to maintain these records.

In the contemporary landscape of digital banking transactions, this record-keeping role is assumed by the bank. The bank, subject to regulatory oversight, ensures transparency about the funds Dori possesses and how she utilizes them. In this context, the bank functions as a third-party entity, independent and responsible for maintaining accurate records.

Nonetheless, it's crucial to remember that digital banking transactions are underpinned by actual, physical banknotes. The quantity and issuance of these banknotes are regulated by the respective central bank. Here, we return to the initial point: the bank resolved the issue of digitally distributing physical banknotes. However, in the second scenario, Dori possesses a digital photo of a banknote. Questions arise: Who captured that photo? How did Dori obtain it? What are her intentions for spending it? Furthermore, uncertainties linger regarding the total number of such digital photos and whether they hold genuine value.

Blockchain digital ledger concept

Blockchain provides a straightforward solution to the scenario involving the digital photo on Dori's phone and the question of record-keeping. Rather than relying on a third party like a bank, trusted friend, or notary, blockchain proposes that the record should be decentralized and shared with everyone interested in sharing digital photos of banknotes through their mobile phones or computers.

In contrast to a centralized model, blockchain introduces a distributed approach. Rather than having a centralized ledger tracking the number of digital photos of $100 on Dori's phone or computer, this information is dispersed among the phones and computers of all participants involved. This includes not only Dori but also Aris and others engaged in exchanging digital photos for $100 via mobile phones or computers. The blockchain diligently records and disseminates this information to everyone. If Dori shares her unique digital photo of $100 with Aris, the blockchain accurately registers an "outflow" from Dori and an "inflow" to Aris, ensuring verification and distribution across the network. Attempting to send the same digital photo to 100 more friends becomes impractical since the blockchain records of all others are not synchronized. In their records, Dori no longer owns a digital photo of $100, leading to the rejection of her attempted transaction. Consequently, Dori no longer possesses the digital photo, while Aris does.

2.1 Distributed and traditional database

Blockchain operates as a decentralized database, recording a comprehensive audit trail of all transactions. Unlike traditional databases, it is managed by a network of computers, with no single computer holding sole responsibility for storage or administration. This ensures that any computer can join or leave the network without compromising data integrity or availability. The database can be restored from scratch by any computer, simply by downloading it from the network and processing the audit trail.

In contrast, traditional databases are typically controlled by a single organization with complete authority, including the ability to manipulate data. While this may not pose issues in certain contexts, the sensitive nature of financial transactions creates a risk of data manipulation and falsification. To counter this, banks undergo continuous audit and regulatory scrutiny, facing persistent threats from external malicious hackers.

Blockchain addresses these challenges by allowing the database to be managed by a distributed network, making it publicly accessible to everyone. This open model enables anyone to create a redundant copy of the database and verify it against other copies. However, this approach is best suited for static data that does not change over time.

For dynamic data, a consensus problem arises when changes are needed after the database has been distributed. Determining the validity, permission, and order of changes becomes crucial. Allowing any entity with a copy of the database to make changes could lead to desynchronization, and a consensus must be reached on which database reflects the true state.

Introducing an entity with the privilege to make changes first, followed by others copying the database, attempts to address this issue. However, this raises concerns of potential data manipulation and censorship by the chosen entity for personal gain. A solution could involve a rotational system for managing entities and copying the "correct" state of the database. Yet, determining the order and process of changing controlling entities remains a question [4].

2.2 Blockchain: the final solution

Blockchain technology addresses these challenges by establishing a network of computers, known as nodes, each of which possesses a copy of the database and adheres to a set of rules defined as a consensus protocol. The consensus protocol outlines the sequence in which nodes can introduce changes to the database, ensuring unanimous agreement among all network nodes regarding the database's state. This structure prevents any single entity from having the authority to manipulate or censor transactions.

Moreover, the blockchain includes an immutable audit trail documenting all modifications to the database. This feature enables all controlling entities to scrutinize and validate the accuracy of the database. The audit trail comprises individual changes referred to as transactions. A set of transactions added to the database by a single node constitutes a "block." Each block contains a reference to the preceding block in the blockchain, establishing a chronological order [4]. The blockchain, essentially a chain of blocks, interconnects each block with the previous one and includes a list of new transactions occurring after the preceding block. When a new node joins the network, it initiates an empty database and retrieves all previous blocks from the network. This process ensures alignment with the databases of all other nodes.

Fundamentally, blockchain orchestrates the sequence of transactions within the database, enabling anyone to verify its accuracy by reconstructing it from the beginning.

2.3 Blockchain in action

Blockchain technology finds widespread application in Bitcoin, a prominent example of its utilization. Bitcoin operates as a digital cryptocurrency, employing blockchain for monitoring transactions and issuing digital currency units.

When an individual intends to spend Bitcoins, they generate a transaction specifying the amount and recipient. This transaction is digitally signed and disseminated to nodes within the Bitcoin network. Upon the creation of the next block in the transaction chain by one of the nodes, it verifies the validity of the new transaction. If deemed valid, the transaction is included in the block, which, as part of the replicated chain, is distributed across all nodes in the network. This process effectively records an outflow from the sender and an inflow to the recipient [5].

2.4 Blockchain consensus protocol

The primary function of a consensus protocol is to establish rules governing the addition of blocks to the chain in terms of order and timing. This is crucial for a blockchain to maintain a consistent and unalterable sequence of events, universally agreed upon by all nodes, representing the current state of the database. Furthermore, this event sequence should be immune to censorship, ensuring that no single node possesses unilateral control over the admission of information. Currently, there are two main types of consensus protocols in use [6]:

2.4.1 Proof of work (PoW)

Proof of Work (PoW) serves as the original consensus protocol within the Bitcoin network. This protocol relies on solving intricate logic puzzles that are challenging to solve but easy to verify once completed. It can be likened to assembling a complex jigsaw puzzle with a multitude of tiny pieces — a formidable task to piece together, but a quick glance can confirm if the picture is complete and accurate. In the PoW protocol, the exertion involved in solving the puzzle is termed "Work," and the puzzle solution is the "Proof of Work." Essentially, the ability to verify the correctness of the solution confirms that someone has performed the work accurately.

A blockchain utilizing a PoW consensus protocol requires proof for each block added to the chain. As a reward for their efforts, the node receives a specific number of digital tokens, characteristic of the network. In the case of the Bitcoin network, this reward is in the form of Bitcoins, constituting the initial generation of these digital tokens. All circulating Bitcoins and those to be released in the future are generated as a reward for the work executed by the nodes in the block generation process, commonly known as "mining." The PoW protocol inherently values the chain with the most blocks as the current "correct" chain, given the greater cumulative work invested in it.

Considered highly secure, the PoW protocol presents a significant challenge for any attempt to overwrite or forge a block. Such an alteration would invalidate previous blocks, requiring the reworking of all prior blocks before a new block could be added. For a successful alteration, a node would need a processing speed exceeding 51% of the combined speed of all other nodes — an event known as a "51% attack." While configuring such a system is currently nearly impossible, the potential rise of quantum computers may necessitate a reevaluation of this blockchain protocol in the future.

2.4.2 Proof of stake (PoS)

Proof of Stake (PoS) represents a more recent consensus protocol model, presently adopted by networks such as Peercoin and BitShares. In contrast to Proof of Work (PoW), the PoS consensus protocol operates on distinct principles unrelated to the high processing power of verification nodes. Instead, preference is granted to nodes with a larger share of the digital (crypto) currency underpinning the process.

Advocates of the PoS protocol argue that nodes possessing a substantial stake in the background cryptocurrency exhibit a heightened interest in preserving its market value. Safeguarding their investment becomes paramount, as any network attack or data falsification would erode trust and, consequently, diminish value. Consequently, it is not in their interest to engage in censorship or the falsification of transactions.

While PoW necessitates substantial processing power, with technologically advanced nodes operating complex puzzle-solving processes in specialized facilities (often termed computer farms), PoS imposes minimal requirements on processing power. This means that even an ordinary smartphone can effectively contribute to the creation of complete blocks. This characteristic significantly enhances the decentralized nature of the network, as a broader range of entities can afford to participate in the validation process.

2.5 Types of blockchain

Blockchain technology is characterized by its openness and accessibility, allowing for diverse implementations based on specific needs. There are essentially three types of blockchain implementations [7]:

i. *Public blockchain:* This type constitutes a fully distributed network that is openly accessible to anyone with internet connectivity. Participants can engage at any level, the program code is open and community-maintained, and the validation process can be undertaken by any participant with the requisite technical equipment. Participants typically remain anonymous. Examples include *Bitcoin* and *Ethereum*.

ii. *Controlled blockchain (permissioned or hybrid blockchain):* In this model, participants assume strictly controlled roles within the network. The validation process is not open to just anyone; instead, it is managed by pre-selected entities. The program code may or may not be available to participants. *Ripple* is an example of a controlled blockchain.

iii. *Private blockchain:* Access to private blockchain networks is meticulously controlled and centrally managed. These networks are closed, permitting entry only to pre-approved participants. The program code is closed and not publicly accessible. Private blockchains find utility in consortia and larger corporations that necessitate sharing information and documents among approved entities. In the financial sector, developing a private blockchain is meant to facilitate back-office operations related to clearing and settlement.

3. The application of blockchain in worldwide financial systems: its advantages and implications!

The intersection of financial systems with information technologies has witnessed a revolutionary shift with the advent of blockchain technology, offering the potential to fundamentally reshape financial landscapes. Several key advantages of blockchain contribute to its transformative impact [8]:

- *Publicly available ledger system*: Blockchain operates as a publicly accessible ledger, where all transactions are recorded and verified. This inherent transparency ensures a secure and reliable system, instilling trust among participants.

- *Transaction immutability:* Every transaction within the blockchain is authorized and validated by controllers known as "miners." Once recorded, transactions become immutable, meaning they cannot be altered or tampered with. This feature enhances security, providing robust protection against malicious intrusions and hacks—common concerns in contemporary financial IT systems.

- *Elimination of intermediaries*: Blockchain technology eliminates the need for intermediaries, enabling direct peer-to-peer transactions. Traditional financial systems often involve intermediaries such as banks or clearinghouses, introducing delays and costs. Blockchain streamlines the process, facilitating more efficient and cost-effective transactions.

- *Decentralization:* One of the core tenets of blockchain is decentralization. This technology is practically available to everyone, fostering a decentralized network where no single entity holds exclusive control. This decentralization not only enhances accessibility but also contributes to the resilience and security of the system.

As blockchain continues to evolve, these advantages pave the way for more inclusive, efficient, and secure financial systems. The elimination of intermediaries, coupled with enhanced transparency and immutability, opens doors to innovative financial applications and services, driving a shift towards more direct and peer-to-peer interactions in the digital economy.

The above-mentioned advantages of blockchain technology are manifested in various ways, particularly within financial systems, bringing about transformative possibilities:

- *Cross-border payments:* Enable fast, direct one-to-one payments, reducing costs for international transactions.

- *Faster and better trading:* Facilitates faster and more extensive trading, addressing constraints in international trade and finance. Allows for the creation of decentralized organizations and micro-investments.

- *Guaranteed payments:* Ensures guaranteed payments, enhancing trade in low-trust countries. Levels the playing field for poorer countries in international trading.

- *Micropayments:* Supports efficient micropayments, reducing fraud risks and transaction costs.

- *Control of payments and prevention of money laundering:* Acts as a decentralized tool for controlling payments and preventing money laundering. Provides a globally accessible ledger for anti-money laundering and anti-terrorist financing.

Despite these benefits, challenges include the risk of fund loss due to hacker attacks, and users bear the responsibility for their security in the absence of a centralized resolution authority. As blockchain continues to evolve, addressing these challenges is crucial for maximizing its impact on financial systems and global trade. Moreover, companies venturing into the implementation of blockchain technology, particularly in its early stages, face a spectrum of risk factors that demand thorough understanding and careful management [8]:

- *Limited major implementations:* Blockchain is a developing technology with a relatively small number of major implementations. The full scope of its limitations is not yet understood and is actively under research. Unanswered questions persist, such as how the model would scale with the substantial volume of daily transactions in financial markets.

- *Transaction cost volatility:* Observations from current implementations, notably with Bitcoin, reveal considerable fluctuations in transaction costs, ranging from minimal to unprofitable. Managing this volatility is crucial, particularly in domains like micropayments, where transaction costs can surpass the value of the payment itself.

- *Rapid evolution of code and implementation methods:* As a developing technology, the programming code and implementation methods are evolving rapidly. Organizations in the early stages of implementation may face risks associated with rule changes, modifications, or discontinuation of support for certain aspects of the technology.

- *Security risks:* Security risks in blockchain technology are multifaceted and demand comprehensive attention. Considerations include access control, the robustness of cryptographic algorithms, the security of control nodes in the network, the potential dominance of processors (e.g., quantum processors), and the risk of denial-of-service attacks leading to potential unavailability.

While these risks are inherent in the current state of blockchain technology, ongoing advancements, research, and industry maturation are expected to mitigate these challenges over the long term. Companies should adopt a proactive approach to risk management and stay abreast of developments to ensure the successful and secure implementation of blockchain solutions.

4. Conclusions

Blockchain, at its core, operates as a decentralized and tamper-resistant digital ledger, offering a transparent and secure way to record and verify transactions. While it initially gained prominence through its association with cryptocurrencies like Bitcoin, the technology's potential extends far beyond the realm of digital money.

In the modern financial industry, blockchain's distributed ledger concept is particularly promising. Traditional financial systems often rely on centralized databases maintained by trusted intermediaries, introducing vulnerabilities to fraud, errors, and data manipulation. Blockchain addresses these challenges by distributing the ledger across a network of nodes, ensuring consensus and transparency. This decentralized nature reduces the dependence on a central authority, fostering trust and integrity in financial transactions.

However, blockchain technology is recognized as a foundational element in the financial sector, offering promising prospects for economic development, financial innovation, and internet advancement. As the financial industry undergoes a digital transformation, successful adoption of blockchain technology becomes imperative. Current research delves into the mediating role of blockchain adoption in the relationship between digital business strategy and process innovation, as well as financial performance. Furthermore, new findings investigate how information technology alignment plays a moderating role in this scenario. The investigation seeks to unveil the nuanced dynamics and interconnections among these crucial components, with the overarching goal of utilizing blockchain for strategic and operational improvements within the financial sector [9]. Moreover, Blockchain technology significantly impacts the financial sector by enhancing security through decentralization and cryptography, leading to efficient processes and reduced costs. Its transparency and traceability improve risk management, support cross-border transactions, and facilitate innovations such as decentralized finance (DeFi) and tokenization. Blockchain ensures regulatory compliance, strengthens data security, and prevents fraud, fostering financial inclusion and revolutionizing traditional financial products and services.

Beyond finance, various industries are exploring blockchain applications. Sectors such as supply chain management, healthcare, real estate, and even governance are considering how blockchain can enhance efficiency, security, and transparency. For instance, in supply chain management, blockchain can enable real-time tracking of products from manufacturing to delivery, reducing fraud and ensuring the authenticity of goods.

However, the adoption of blockchain technology comes with its share of challenges and risks. Issues such as scalability, regulatory uncertainties, and the environmental impact of certain consensus mechanisms (like Proof of Work) are subjects of ongoing discussion and exploration. It is crucial for organizations to carefully evaluate their specific use cases and consider the potential risks associated with implementing blockchain solutions.

Moreover, blockchain should not be seen as a one-size-fits-all solution. Each industry and business process affected by blockchain requires a thoughtful examination of whether the technology can address existing weaknesses or inefficiencies. While blockchain holds tremendous promise, successful implementation requires a comprehensive understanding of its capabilities, limitations, and the unique requirements of each use case.

As the technology continues to mature, ongoing research, development, and collaboration among industries, regulators, and technology innovators will contribute to unlocking the full potential of blockchain in reshaping the way we manage, secure, and share data across various sectors.

Author details

Artina Bedjeti Baftijari* and Leonid Nakov
Faculty of Economics, University St. Cyril and Methodius, Skopje, North Macedonia

*Address all correspondence to: artinabexheti@hotmail.com

References

[1] Banerjee A. An in-depth look at blockchain technology: Architecture and security concerns. In: Distributed Computing to Blockchain. London: Elsevier; 2023. pp. 297-325

[2] Binariks. 2023. [Online]. Available from: https://binariks.com/blog/emerging-blockchain-technology-trends/. [Accessed: December 28, 2023]

[3] Begum A, Tareq AH, Sultana M, Sohel MK. Blockchain attacks analysis and a model to solve double spending attack. International Journal of Machine Learning and Computing. 2020;**10**(2):352-357

[4] Meunier S. Blockchain 101: What is blockchain and how does this revolutionary technology work. In: Transforming Climate Finance and Green Investment with Blockchains. London: Elsevier; 2018. pp. 23-34

[5] PwC. [Online]. Available from: https://www.pwc.com/us/en/industries/financial-services/fintech/bitcoin-blockchain-cryptocurrency.html. [Accessed: December 15, 2023]

[6] Judmayer A, Stifter N, Krombholz K, Weippl E. Blocks and Chains: Introduction to Bitcoin, Cryptocurrencies, and their Consensus Mechanisms. Berlin: Springer Nature; 2022

[7] Seth S. Investopedia. 2023. [Online]. Available from: https://www.investopedia.com/news/public-private-permissioned-blockchains-compared/ [Accessed: December 20, 2023]

[8] Tamplin T. Finance Strategists. 2023. [Online]. Available from: https://www.financestrategists.com/wealth-management/blockchain/blockchain-advantages-and-disadvantages/. [Accessed: December 08, 2023]

[9] Khalil M, Khawaja KF, Sarfraz M. The adoption of blockchain technology in the financial sector during the era of fourth industrial revolution: A moderated mediated model. Quality & Quantity. 2022;**56**(4):2435-2452

Chapter 5

Modelling Extreme Tail Risk of Bitcoin Returns Using the Generalised Pareto Distribution

Providence Mushori and Delson Chikobvu

Abstract

This paper analyses the extreme tail behaviour of Bitcoin returns by fitting a Generalised Pareto Distribution (GPD). The GPD is used to model the extreme daily Bitcoin returns over the period 2008 to 2023. The returns above the chosen thresholds, for both Bitcoin gains and losses, are selected. The GPD is then fitted to the selected excess returns. The Anderson Darling (AD) and Kolmogorov Smirnov (K-S) goodness-of-fit tests reveal that the GPD captures the distribution of the Bitcoin excess returns. The Value at Risk (VaR) and Expected Shortfall (ES) under the GPD are used to measure the extreme tail risk of the Bitcoin returns. The upside risk (gains) is found to outweigh downside risk (losses), and this gives insight to investors interested in Bitcoin.

Keywords: generalised Pareto distribution (GPD), value at risk (VaR), expected shortfall (ES), bitcoin, tail risk

1. Introduction

Predicting the likelihood of an extreme event within a given period is often reflected in the volatility of that event. Statistical methods have proved effective in forecasting extreme movements of financial events, and in this case, focus is given to Bitcoin extreme price index movements. A Generalised Pareto Distribution (GPD) is a family of continuous probability distributions which falls under extreme value theory (EVT) [1]. Ever since the EVT was developed in the 1920s, it has been used to predict the occurrence of several different extreme events including financial market crashes and other black swan events [2, 3]. EVT has been applied to the crypto currency market to predict cryptocurrency price movements using the Generalised Extreme Value distribution [4]. The aim of this paper is to show how the EVT based GPD models extreme Bitcoin gains and losses and assessing the risk levels thereof.

2. Review of literature

Bitcoin, for several years, has had the largest market share in the crypto industry. Evidence in the literature suggests that much research has been done on Bitcoin [5–9].

IntechOpen

Research done by Osterrieder and Lorenz [10] showed Bitcoin extreme price changes to be violating the usual normal distribution assumption. The selection of an appropriate statistical distribution to asset returns becomes the challenge. Osterrieder and Lorenz [10] conducted a study on the extreme tail behaviour of Bitcoin where he performed an in-depth extreme univariate analysis. Bitcoin was found to exhibit volatility that was higher than the Group of 10 (G10) countries' currencies. The G10 countries comprise of Belgium, Canada, France, Germany, Italy, Japan, the Netherlands, Sweden, Switzerland, the United Kingdom and the United States. Non-normality and heavier tails were observed to be stronger in Bitcoin prices, in comparison to the G10 countries' currencies. In extreme value analysis, there are two approaches to selecting extremes, and these are the block maxima and the peaks-over threshold methods [11]. Islam and Pial Das [7] conducted a study on predicting Bitcoin returns using Extreme Value Theory (EVT). Extreme Bitcoin returns were modelled using the block maxima and the peak over threshold approaches. It was concluded that Bitcoin extreme tail distributions are well represented by the EVT based distributions and that investors can make use of the results of their findings. The authors used return levels as measures of risk. This paper uses the Basel III recommended Value at Risk (VaR) to quantify risk. VaR is used in quantifying minimum capital requirements. The Expected Shortfall (ES) is also used in this paper to quantify extreme risk in Bitcoin on this updated dataset. Moreover, this paper separates gains from losses in the analysis.

Cryptocurrencies are considered highly volatile and show extreme tail movements when compared to traditional financial markets and fiat currencies [12, 13]. In this study, research is conducted on the Bitcoin extreme gains and losses by fitting the GPD. Risk analysis measures, such as VaR and ES are computed on the Bitcoin extreme returns. The peaks over threshold based GPD is chosen over the block maxima based Generalised Extreme Value Distribution (GEVD) as the former makes use of the data more efficiently.

This research extends EVT applications by fitting the GPD and in quantifying the extreme volatile behaviour of Bitcoin log returns using the VaR and the ES as measures of risk.

3. Methodology

This section describes the methods and tools that are used in the study. The properties of empirical distribution used in the analysis of the returns are also explained. Descriptions of the criteria that are used in the data selection process and in the goodness of fit tests on the extreme tails of the Bitcoin returns are explained as well. The GPD is applied on the Bitcoin extreme price returns data in order to analyse the tail behaviour of Bitcoin extreme returns. The threshold selection methods to be applied to the Bitcoin returns data are also discussed. The returns are defined as:

$$z_t = \log\left(\frac{P_t}{P_{t-1}}\right) = \log(P_t) - \log(P_{t-1}), \tag{1}$$

where P_t represents the price of Bitcoin at time t and P_{t-1} represents the price at time $t-1$.

DOI: http://dx.doi.org/10.5772/intechopen.1003794

3.1 Data selection process

The data used in the study are taken from CoinMarketCap "Cryptocurrency Market Capitalizations" and retrieved from https://coinmarketcap.com/ on September 01 of 2023. The data is of the period 28 April 2013 to 1 September 2023. There are four data sets for Bitcoin prices considered, which are the daily opening prices, daily closing prices, daily low and daily high prices. The Bitcoin daily closing price data were finally chosen for carrying out the analysis. Any of the 4 data sets could have been used since they all had similar descriptive statistics features. The Bitcoin daily closing prices used in this study are an average of the closing price values from several Bitcoin exchanges.

3.2 Extreme value theory (EVT) – peak over threshold

The peaks-over-threshold (PoT) analysis, also known as the partial durations series analysis in some more applied fields, has played a fundamental role in the development of statistical EVT. It is based on fitting a GPD to the data exceedances above a large enough threshold.

3.3 Generalised Pareto distribution (GPD)

The GPD emerges from the EVT. It models values of a given random variable that are above a certain threshold value. Threshold simply means a point on a statistical distribution above which values can be taken as extreme. The data used for a GPD can be ordered from the smallest observed excess to the highest observed excess. The excess of the values observed above the threshold is also known as the exceedances and are peaks over a threshold. For instance, if there is an ordered set of values of a random variable such that Z is $z_1, z_2, z_3, \ldots, z_{n-1}, z_n.$, where z_n is the largest of the values of Z, then the peaks over threshold or excesses/exceedances are denoted as $x_i = z_i - \mu$.

The data of the exceedances is known to follow the GPD and with a probability density function of the form:

$$f(z_i;\beta,\gamma) = \begin{cases} \dfrac{1}{\beta}\left(1+\gamma\left(\dfrac{z_i-\mu}{\beta}\right)^{-\frac{1}{\gamma}-1}\right) & \text{for } \gamma \neq 0 \\ \dfrac{1}{\beta}\exp\left(\dfrac{\mu - z_i}{\beta}\right) & \text{for } \gamma = 0, \end{cases} \tag{2}$$

where μ is the threshold value, β is the scale parameter and γ is the shape parameter.

From Eq. (2) a corresponding Cumulative Distribution Function (CDF) for the GPD is derived and is given as:

$$F(z_i;\beta,\gamma) = \begin{cases} 1 - \left(1 + \dfrac{\gamma(z_i-\mu)}{\beta}\right)^{-\frac{1}{\gamma}} & \text{for } z \in [u,\infty] \text{ and } \gamma \neq 0 \\ 1 - \exp\left(-\dfrac{(z_i-\mu)}{\beta}\right) & \text{for } z \in [u,\infty] \text{ and } \gamma = 0 \end{cases} \tag{3}$$

From Eq. (3), if z follows the GPD (γ, β), then $z + \mu$ is a GPD ($\gamma, \beta + \mu\gamma$), given that $z > \mu$ for any threshold value μ. It also implies that $z - \mu$, provided $z > \mu$, follows a GPD ($\gamma, \beta - \mu\gamma$). Castillo and Hadi [14] stipulated that consistence of a model with a data set goes hand in hand with the model being consistent with the same data set for all high threshold values. Another interesting fact about the GPD is that, for a certain range of values for γ, the GPD reduces to certain types of common distributions.

The following cases show a resulting distribution from a GPD when the parameter γ takes certain values:

Case 1: when $\gamma = 0$, the GPD reduces to a two-parameter exponential distribution with a mean denoted by β. This distribution is often described as light tailed.

Case 2: when $\gamma \leq -0.5$, its variance is equal to ∞, meaning that if $\gamma > -\frac{1}{n}$, and then the nth central moment exists.

Case 3: if $\gamma < 0$, the GPD becomes a Pareto type II distribution which has a bounded tail.

Case 4: when $\gamma = 1$, the GPD reduces to a uniform distribution U $[0, \beta]$.

Case 5: when $\gamma > 0$, the GPD becomes an ordinary heavy tailed Pareto distribution.

3.4 Threshold selection for the GPD

Adopting a low threshold value results in sensible approximations to the peaks-over threshold for the GPD with a relatively large sample size [15]. Lower threshold values give an advantage of credibility especially in cases where the main body of data is not sufficient for analysis. However, the theory of convergence to the GPD may not hold and often results in bias in such cases. Too large of a threshold result in fewer observations with a high variance in parameter estimation. The high variance is a result of having fewer extreme values caused by a selection of this very high threshold. Hence a good threshold value is chosen such that a balance should be achieved between variance and bias. There are several threshold selection methods but only three are used in this study, and these are the Pareto Q-Q plot, the mean excess plot and the parameter stability plot. Graphs in **Figure 1** show the peaks-over thresholds

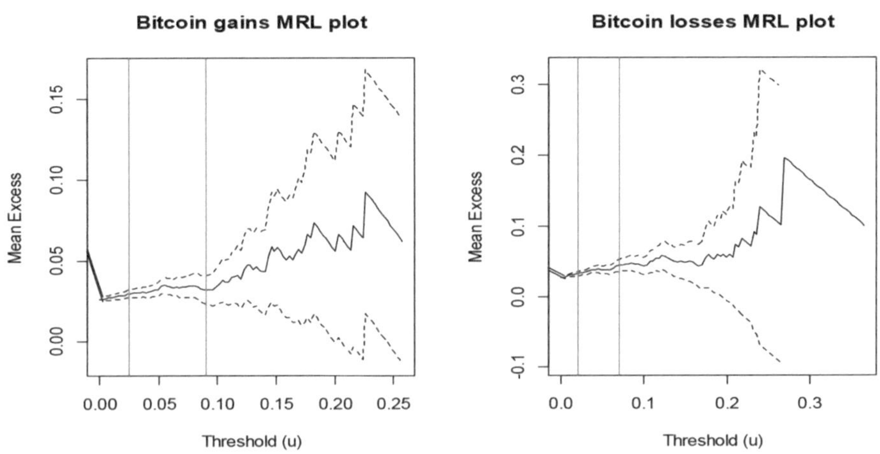

Figure 1.
Mean residual live plot of bitcoin positive and negative returns.

selection methods for the Bitcoin gains and losses data respectively. Losses are negative returns turned to positive values by multiplying with a negative one. This is done for easier analysis and distribution fitting.

3.5 Mean excess plots

The main idea behind the mean excess plots is to find the extent to which an observed value z exceeds a certain extrema threshold value given that the observed value is greater than the threshold value, μ. In mathematical terms, the mean excess equation is denoted as:

$$e(\mu) = E(Z - \mu | Z > \mu). \tag{4}$$

For a set of independent extreme events, the mean excess is defined as the mean of all the values above the threshold, provided the values are arranged in order such that the last is the maximum. If $z_1, z_2, z_3, \ldots, z_{n-1}, z_n$ are the values of the variable Z arranged in order, then z_n would be the maximum. This method is carried out at 95% confidence level such that the expected threshold value is found to be lying in the expected confidence interval. Observing a straight positive gradient from bottom left to top right depicts a fat tailed GPD that has a positive shape parameter. If the gradient of the slope is negative, then the mean excess plot depicts or indicates a thin-tailed behaviour. The mean residual plots for the Bitcoin gains and losses are shown **Figure 1**.

Based on the two graphs in **Figure 1**, the threshold is favourably stable between 0.02 and 0.08 for both the Bitcoin gains returns and the Bitcoin losses as shown by the green lines on the graphs above, therefore the threshold value is most likely to be between the values 0.02 and 0.08.

3.6 Pareto Q-Q plot

The Pareto Q-Q plot method pinpoints the threshold and involves fitting a regression line to the data points in the Pareto Q-Q plot. It is possible to check whether a model is plausible enough to be a good fit for the data. The Q-Q plots are easy to compute, especially for the exponential distribution [16]. The point where the fitted tangent regression line cuts the y-axis (z-axis in this instance) is used to calculate the threshold value in the data set. The exponent of the value where the regression line cuts through the y-axis (z-axis) is taken as the threshold value. The green dotted line in the two graphs in **Figure 2** shows the regression line.

The threshold values for the Bitcoin gains and for the Bitcoin losses are observed to be approximately equal to the exponent of -3.5 and -3.7 respectively, corresponding to 0.03 and 0.025 respectively. The Q-Q plots for the Bitcoin price returns for gains and losses are shown in **Figure 2**.

Based on **Figure 2**, threshold values of 0.03 and 0.025 are selected for gains and losses respectively (after rounding to three decimal places), and 578 and 613 exceedances are obtained for gains and losses respectively. The parameter stability plots for gains are in **Figure 3a**.

The parameter stability estimate plots in **Figure 3a** and **b**, support the reasonable and suggested thresholds from the pareto Q-Q plots of 0.0302 and 0.0247 for Bitcoin gains and losses respectively, since stability is observed at around these threshold values. The same can be said of the results from the mean residual live plots.

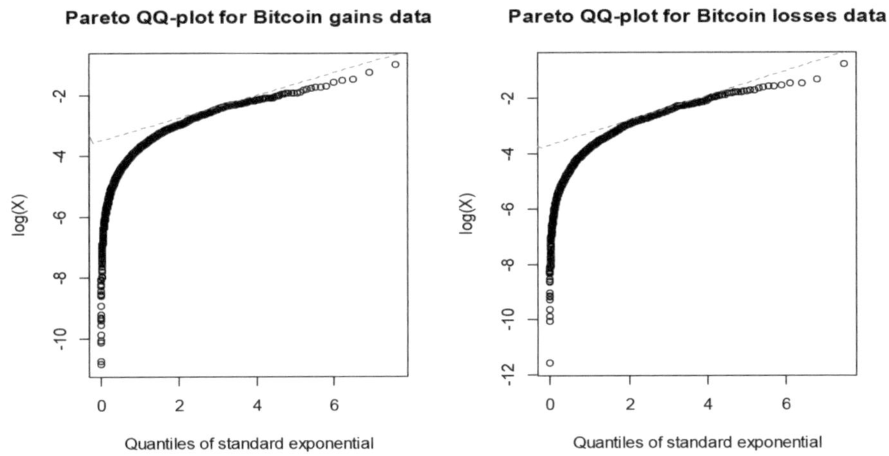

Figure 2.
Q-Q plots for bitcoin positive and negative log returns.

3.7 Risk measures

Risk measures used in this study are the VaR and ES.

3.8 Value at risk (VaR)

The VaR refers to the maximum amount of potential loss on a security or a portfolio over a period, with a given degree of confidence. In other words, it generalises the probability of underperforming by providing a statistical measure of downside risk. VaR can be in two forms, depending on the state of the data or distribution being considered. We will only look at the continuous case since the distribution of Bitcoin gains and losses data is continuous in nature. For a continuous random variable Z, VaR is defined as:

$$\text{VaR(Z)} = -t \text{ where } P(Z < t) = p. \tag{5}$$

VaR is measured based on assumptions that may not be apparent on immediate terms. In most practical terms, normality is assumed. It is known that securities or portfolios exposed to systematic bias, credit risk or derivatives may not exhibit normality [17]. In such circumstances, the usefulness of VaR would depend on modelling the skewness of the returns data in the form of the GPD or via monte carlo simulations. The fatter the tail, the more lacking the data is in the very extremities.

3.9 VaR in extreme value using GPD

The VaR for the GPD is computed as:

$$\widehat{VaR} = \begin{cases} \mu + \frac{\hat{\beta}}{\hat{\gamma}}\left\{\left(\frac{n}{N_\mu}p\right)^{-\gamma} - 1\right\} & \hat{\gamma} \neq 0 \\ \mu - \hat{\beta}\log\left(\frac{n}{N_\mu}(1-p)\right) & \hat{\gamma} = 0 \end{cases} \tag{6}$$

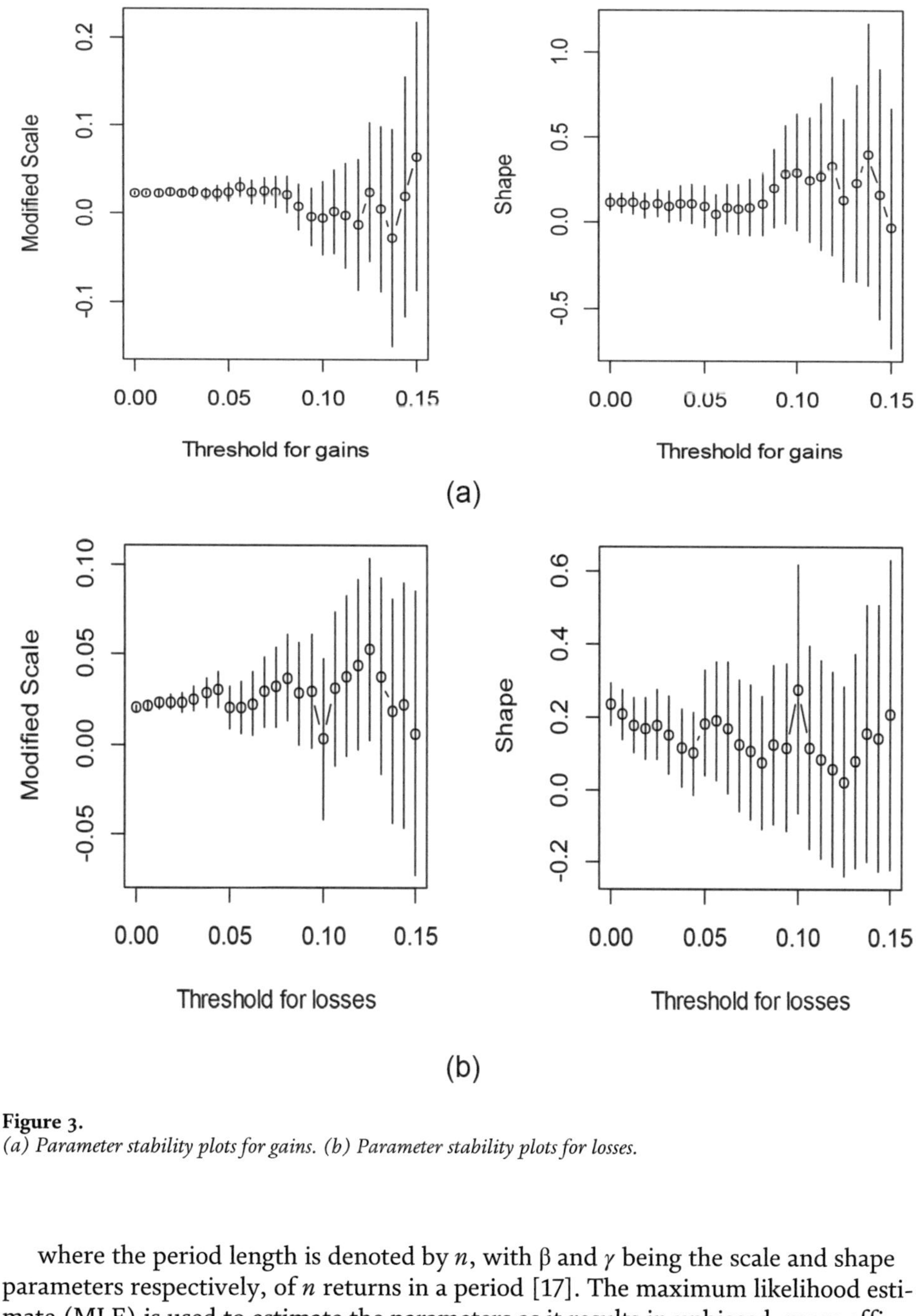

Figure 3.
(a) Parameter stability plots for gains. (b) Parameter stability plots for losses.

where the period length is denoted by n, with β and γ being the scale and shape parameters respectively, of n returns in a period [17]. The maximum likelihood estimate (MLE) is used to estimate the parameters as it results in unbiased, more efficient, and minimum variance estimators. The variable p denotes the probability of the small upper tail.

3.10 Expected shortfall (ES)

The ES is the average of all the returns in a distribution that are worse than VaR of the portfolio at a given level of confidence. For example, for a 95% confidence level,

ES is obtained by taking the average of returns in the worst 5% of cases. It provides a return expected that exceed VaR for a given level of probability. In a general continuous case, the ES is given as:

$$\text{ES} = E[\max(L - Z, 0)] = \int_{-\infty}^{L} (L - Z)f(z)dz, \tag{7}$$

where L is the chosen benchmark level. In a general discrete case, the ES is given by:

$$\text{ES} = E[\,max\,(L - Z, 0)] = \sum\nolimits_{z<L} (L - z)P(Z = z). \tag{8}$$

In extreme value for the GPD, ES = $VaR_p + E(Z - VaR_p|Z > VaR_p)$, where VaR_p represents the threshold given value.

4. Results and discussion

The calculated thresholds are used to find the exceedances/excesses in fitting the GPD to the losses and gains.

4.1 GPD for the bitcoin losses data

The Bitcoin losses which are above the chosen threshold of 0.025 are used in the analysis using the GPD. The GPD is fitted, and the parameter estimates are found through the MLE approach. This threshold value is obtained from the Q-Q plot and other threshold selection methods used in the previous section. The maximum likelihood estimates for both the shape parameter γ and scale parameter β are observed to be approximately 0.1796 and 0.0271 respectively. Since the confidence interval of the shape parameter γ is greater than 0 at the 95% level of significance, it means that the GPD reduces to a type two Pareto distribution. Thus, a heavy tailed Pareto type two distribution can be used to model the Bitcoin losses. However, we begin by finding if the Bitcoin data can be modelled by the GPD. **Figure 4** shows the likelihood function of both the scale and shape parameters.

It can be seen from **Figure 4** that the shape parameter γ has a value of 0.1796 with a calculated standard error of 0.0499, whereas the scale parameter β has a value of 0.0271 with standard error 0.0017. The shape parameter is above 0, and this means that tail losses are heavier than implied by the normal distribution tail. As a result, extreme losses may occur than anticipated if the data was normally distributed.

Figure 5 shows the model diagnostic plots for the GPD fit to the Bitcoin losses.

The plots in **Figure 5** show that the model is a good fit to the data since most of the data points are collinear and inclined at 45° to the horizontal on the Q-Q plot. The density plot also shows the same evidence as that provided by the Q-Q plot. Therefore, it is concluded that the GPD model is a good fit. A further analysis is done by testing the following hypotheses:

H_0 : The Bitcoin losses follow the GPD.

H_a : The Bitcoin losses do not follow the given GPD.

The results of the tests, using maximum likelihood estimation, are given in **Table 1**.

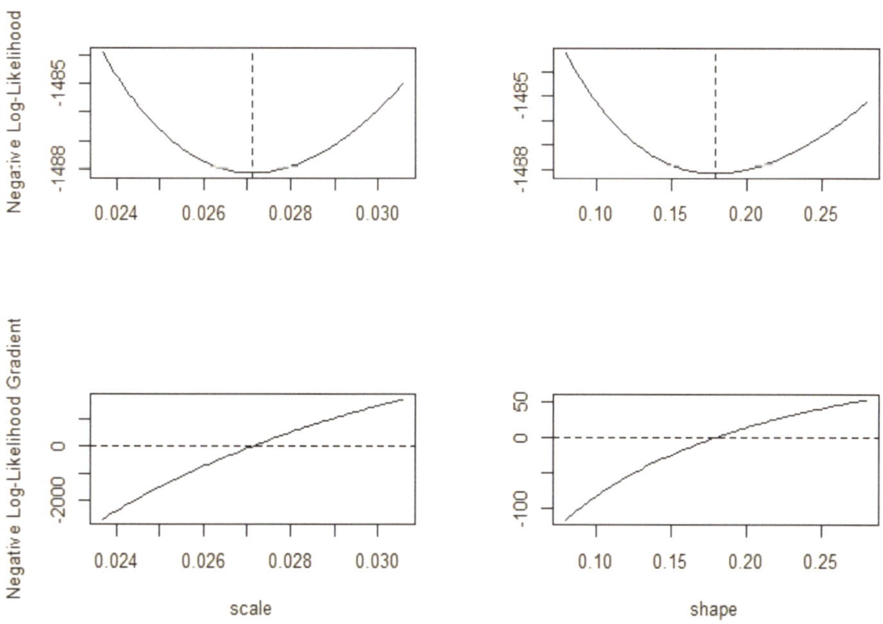

Figure 4.
Maximum likelihood estimation of scale and shape parameters of losses under GPD.

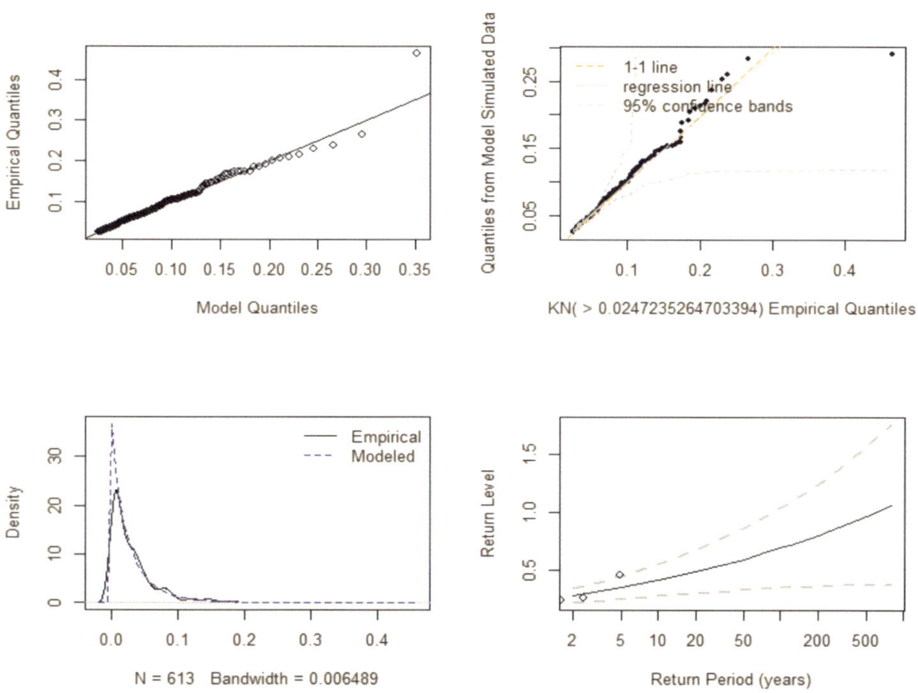

Figure 5.
Density and return plots for the GPD on bitcoin losses data.

Table 1 results show that the Bitcoin losses follow a GPD since the p-values are large and hence there is not enough evidence to reject the null hypothesis.

GPD	AD statistic	AD p-value	K-S statistic	K-S p-value
Negative bitcoin returns	0.4871	0.76	0.0058	0.8895

Table 1.
Tests on goodness-of-fit of the GPD.

4.2 GPD for the bitcoin gains data

The Bitcoin gains data over the chosen threshold of 0.03 are used to find out if the GPD can be a good fit to the data, and parameter estimates are found using the MLE approach. This threshold value is derived from evidence given by the Pareto Q-Q plot and other methods used. The log likelihood estimated values for both the shape parameter γ and scale parameter β are observed to be 0.0842 and 0.0278 respectively.

Figure 6 shows the likelihood functions for both the scale and shape parameters.

Figure 6 shows that the shape parameter γ has a value of 0.0842 and the calculated standard error is 0.0433. The scale parameter is 0.0278 with standard error of 0.0017. **Figure** 7 shows model diagnostic plots for the GPD fit to the Bitcoin gains data above the threshold of 0.0302. The shape parameter is above 0, and this means that the left tail is heavier than the normal distribution tail. As result, extreme gains are more probable to occur.

The plots in **Figure** 7 show that the model is a good fit to the data points using the GPD. From the Q-Q plot (top left), there is a strong indication of linearity for most of the data points. Moving from left to right, the largest quantiles divert from the 45° reference line with few values in the extreme top right. One can still say that the GPD is a good fit for the gains. The top right plot in **Figure** 7 shows the quantiles from a sample drawn from the fitted GPD against the empirical data quantiles with 95% confidence

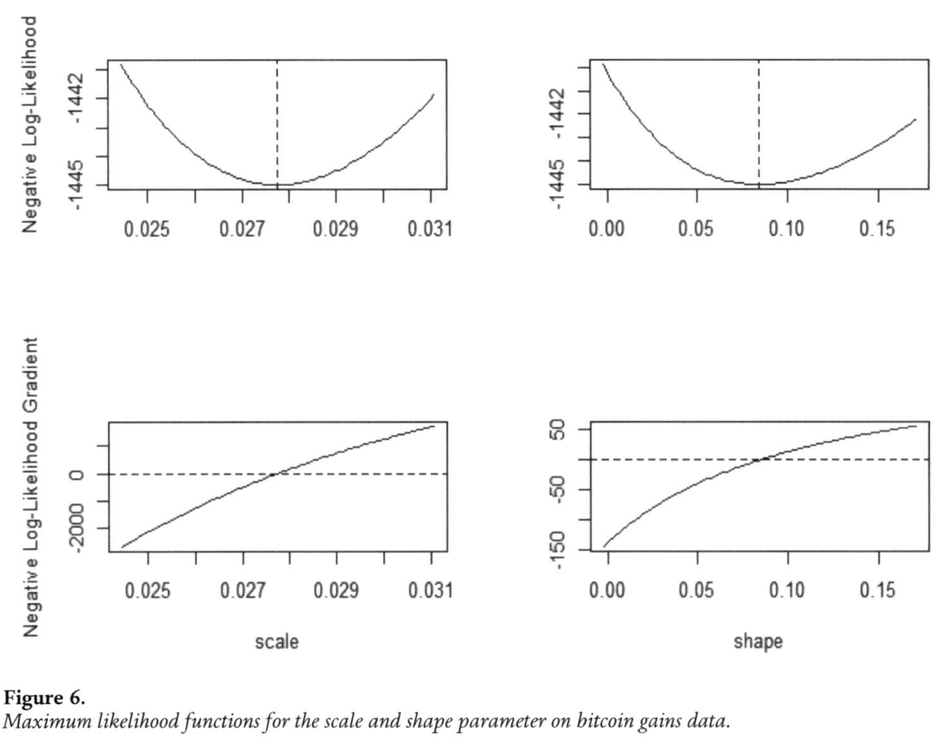

Figure 6.
Maximum likelihood functions for the scale and shape parameter on bitcoin gains data.

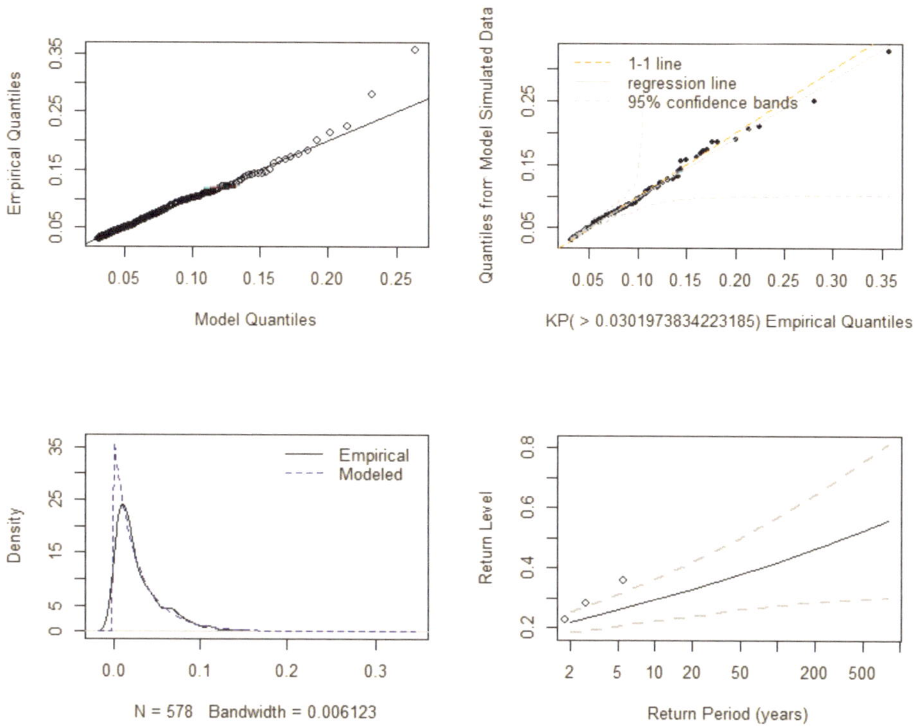

Figure 7.
Diagnostic plots for the GPD fit to the bitcoin gains data above the threshold of 0.03.

bands in dashed lines. Most of the quantiles (black dots) align with the 45°line dashed orange and fall in the confidence bands, which makes for a reasonable GPD fit.

The GPD density function (dashed blue) is overlaid on the empirical density in the bottom left plot and there are some similarities in kurtosis as is in the case for losses.

The return level plot is shown on the bottom right with 95% confidence intervals for the 5-year return level of the logarithm returns of monthly data. Therefore, it can be said at 95% confidence level, that the logarithmic returns will be above the range 0.2 to 0.3, at 95% confidence level.

However, we further investigate the goodness-of-fit of the GPD on Bitcoin gains data by carrying out a goodness of fit test on the following hypotheses:

H_0 : The Bitcoin gains data follow the GPD.

H_a : The Bitcoin gains data do not follow the GPD.

Table 2 gives the results of the test.

It is evident that Bitcoin gains data follow a GPD as shown by the AD and K-S statistics since the p values are greater than 0.05. It follows that an ordinary Pareto distribution can be a good fit since γ is greater than 0 at 5% significance level. Two risk

GPD	AD statistic	AD p-value	K-S statistic	K-S p-value
Gains	0.3730	0.8751	0.0055	0.9202

Table 2.
Tests on goodness-of-fit of the GPD on bitcoin gains data.

Alpha (probability)	0.1	0.05	0.01
Gains	0.0581	0.0735	0.1060
Losses	0.0512	0.0628	0.0850

Table 3.
VaR results.

Alpha (Probability)	0.1	0.05	0.01
Gains	0.0792	0.0934	0.1233
Losses	0.0664	0.0763	0.0950

Table 4.
ES results.

measures, VaR and ES, are applied to the data on gains and losses. The risk values obtained are shown in **Tables 3** and **4**.

4.3 Measures of risk from the GPD

Gains are riskier than losses as the gains are associated with higher values of VaR.

Gains are confirmed to riskier than losses in **Table 4** as the gains are associated with higher values ES.

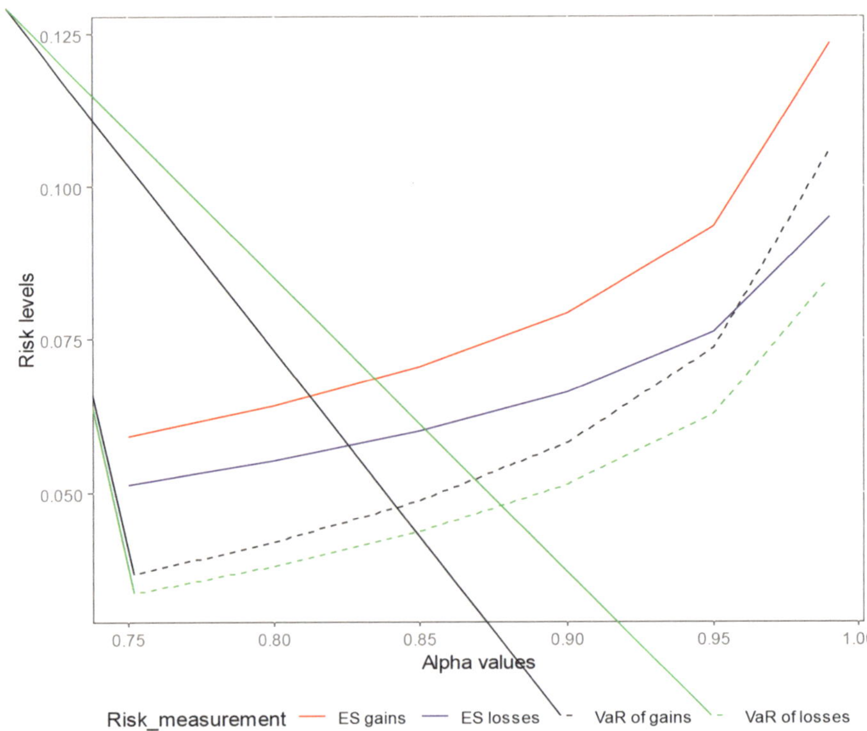

Figure 8.
GPD VaR and ES values to the bitcoin gains and losses returns data.

The GPD VaR and ES values at 99% confidence level are 0.1060 and 0.1233 for the gains, and 0.0850 and 0.0950 for the losses respectively. The interpretation of the upper tail risk values is that the expected gain in the Bitcoin market has a 99% likelihood that it will not exceed 0.1060 but if it does exceed, it will come to an average of 0.1233. The interpretation of the losses risk value is that the expected loss in the Bitcoin market has a 99% likelihood that it will not exceed 0.0850 but if it does exceed, it will come to an average of 0.0950. Analogously, the VaR and ES values, at different probability levels, are explained in the same way.

The **Figure 8** shows the risk measurement values on Bitcoin market returns from 75% confidence level to as much as 99% confidence level. The risk values are plotted against the alpha probability values. It is clearly that the gains have a higher VaR and ES than the losses. In other words, gains seem to outweigh losses, and this can have a good implication to interested investors in Bitcoin, especially the risk seeking investors, in exploring the possibility of higher returns whilst minimising losses. At all alpha values, the VaR and ES of gains are greater than the corresponding values for losses. It is possible to net in those extreme gains. The losses would be smaller is they were to occur.

5. Conclusion

Bitcoin extreme returns were analysed using the GPD. The method of parameter estimation used is the MLE. The GPD is fitted to the peaks over threshold data for the two data sets, viz.: gains and losses. The diagnostics of the model, including goodness-of-fit tests indicators, the AD and K-S tests, confirm the returns data are well modelled using the GPD. The evidence gathered from the descriptive statistics, diagnostic plots, Q-Q plots, pp-plots, and other statistical tools used, show that the GPD is a good fit to the Bitcoin losses and gains data. The VaR and ES values for the gains are higher than those for losses which implies that the possibility of higher gains outweighs the losses when invested in Bitcoin. These results give insight to investors interested in Bitcoin.

Author details

Providence Mushori* and Delson Chikobvu
University of the Free State, Bloemfontein, South Africa

*Address all correspondence to: providencemushori@gmail.com

References

[1] Anderson K, Brooks C. Extreme returns from extreme value stocks. The Journal of Investing. 2007;**16**(1):69-81

[2] Berning TL. Improved estimation procedures for a positive extreme value index [PhD thesis]. Stellenbosch University; 2010

[3] Wadsworth J, Tawn J. Likelihood-based procedures for threshold diagnostics and uncertainty in extreme value modelling. Journal of the Royal Statistical Society: Series B (Statistical Methodology). 2012;**74**(3): 543-567

[4] Guillou A, Kratz M, Strat Y. An extreme value theory approach for the early detection of time clusters. A simulation-based assessment and an illustration to the surveillance of Salmonella. Statistics in Medicine. 2014; **33**(28):5015-5027

[5] Cheah E-T, Fry J. Speculative bubbles in bitcoin markets? An empirical investigation into the fundamental value of bitcoin. Economics Letters. 2015;**130**: 32-36

[6] Dyhrberg AH. Bitcoin, gold and the dollar – A GARCH volatility analysis. Finance Research Letters. 2016;**16**:85-92

[7] Islam MT, Pial Das K. Predicting bitcoin return using extreme value theory. American Journal of Mathematical and Management Sciences. 2021;**40**(2):177-187

[8] Katsiampa P. Volatility estimation for bitcoin: A comparison of GARCH models. Economics Letters. 2017;**158**:3-6

[9] Urquhart A. The inefficiency of bitcoin. Economics Letters. 2016;**148**: 80-82

[10] Osterrieder J, Lorenz J. A statistical risk assessment of bitcoin and its extreme tail behavior. Annual Financial Economics. 2017;**12**:1-13

[11] Dekkers A, Haan L. On the estimation of the extreme-value index and large quantile estimation. The Annals of Statistics. 1989;**17**(4): 1795-1832

[12] Katsiampa P. Volatility co-movement between Bitcoin and Ether. Finance Research Letters. 2019b;**30**: 221-227

[13] Omari C, Ngunyi A. The predictive performance of extreme value analysis based models in forecasting the volatility of cryptocurrencies. Journal of Mathematical Finance. 2021;**11**(03): 438-465

[14] Castillo E, Hadi A. Fitting the generalized Pareto distribution to data. Journal of the American Statistical Association. 1997;**92**(440):1609-1620

[15] Barakat H, Omar A, Khaled O. A new flexible extreme value model for modeling the extreme value data, with an application to environmental data. Statistics & Probability Letters. 2017; **130**:25-31

[16] Beirlant J, Goegebeur Y, Teugels J, Segers J. Statistics of Extremes: Theory and Applications, Wiley Series in Probability and Statistics. Chichester: John Wiley & Sons, Ltd; 2004

[17] Tsay RS. Analysis of Financial Time Series. Wiley Series in Probability and Statistics. Hoboken, NJ: Wiley; 2005

Chapter 6

The Inclusion of Bitcoin and Other Cryptocurrencies in Investors' Portfolios

Prosper Lamothe-López, Prosper Lamothe-Fernández and Leslie Rodríguez-Valencia

Abstract

Cryptocurrencies have become an attractive asset class for all types of investors. A relevant question is whether their inclusion in portfolios improves their risk-return output. In this chapter, we conduct an empirical study of the effect of the inclusion of Bitcoin and Ethereum in the portfolio of a European investor. Additionally, we analyze the results of previous studies on this question under other assumptions. The empirical data are overwhelming regarding the attractiveness of Bitcoin and by extension other cryptocurrencies as an asset class. The important question is whether this appeal is temporary and will eventually disappear so investors do not have to worry about this new asset class. In the chapter we discuss this issue.

Keywords: cryptocurrency, portfolio performance, diversification, Bitcoin, Ethereum

1. Introduction

One of the initial issues we must address when analyzing cryptocurrencies as an investment alternative is whether they represent a new asset class. Following Greer [1], asset classes can be classified as shown in **Table 1**."

In his analysis, Greer distinguishes three broad categories of asset classes: capital assets, consumable/transformable assets, and store-of-value assets. In **Table 1**, traditional asset classes are classified within these three categories.

Based on Greer's work, Burniske and White [2] list the four factors that define the boundaries between different asset classes:

- Investment possibilities.
- Economic and financial characteristics.
- Correlation of returns with other asset classes.
- Risk-return trade-off.

Categorization of traditional asset classes by their superclass			
	Capital assets	**Consumable/ transformable assets**	**Store of value assets**
	"Ongoing source of something of value ... valued on the basis of net present value of its expected returns."	"You can consume it. You can transform it into another asset. It has economic value. But it does not yield an ongoing stream of value."	"Cannot be consumed; nor can it generate income. Nevertheless, it has value; it is a store of value asset."
Equities	X		
Bonds	X		
Income-producing real estate	X		
Physical commodities (e.g., grains or energy products)		X	
Precious metals (e g., Gold)		X	X
Currency			X
Fine art			X

Table 1.
Categorization of traditional asset classes by their superclass.

Investment possibilities[1] refer to the ease and costs involved in buying or selling a particular asset class. These possibilities depend on the liquidity of the instrument, the existence of multiple instruments in the market that allow you to acquire or expose yourself to the asset class, transaction costs in operations, etc.

The liquidity of transactions in Bitcoins and other cryptocurrencies has continually increased since their creation.

On the other hand, investing in cryptocurrencies and/or acquiring exposure to cryptocurrencies is very easy and inexpensive due to the availability of various instruments that allow direct or "virtual" purchase of these assets, such as:

- Cryptocurrency-referenced ETFs.
- Cryptocurrency-referenced CFDs.
- Cryptocurrency investment funds, etc.
- Futures and options with cryptocurrencies as underlying assets.

Regarding investment *via* ETFs, **Table 2** shows the characteristics of the most popular ones in the market according to the Bitcoin Market Journal.

[1] Investability as termed by Burniske and White.

ETF name	Ticker	Exchange	Type	Fees (%)
The VanEck Vectors Bitcoin ETN	VBTC	Deutsche Böerse Xetra	Spot	2
The Bitcoin Investment Trust from Grayscale	GBTC (*on the OTCQX ticker)*	Off-exchange, via registered dealers	Spot	2
XBT Provider ETN	CXBTF	Nasdaq Stockholm Stock Exchange	Spot	2.5
WisdomTree Bitcoin ETP	BTCW	SIX Swiss Exchange	Spot	0.95
CI Galaxy Bitcoin ETF	BTCX	Toronto Stock Exchange	Spot	0.45
Source: Bitcoin Market Journal				

Table 2.
ETFS about Bitcoin.

Contract unit	5 bitcoin, as defined by the CMECF Bitcoin Reference Rate [BRR]
Minimum price fluctuation	Outright: $5.00 per bitcoin = $25.00 per contract Calendar Spread: $1.00 per bitcoin = $5.00 per contract
	CME Globex: Sunday–Friday 6:00 p.m. – 5:00 p.m. ET (5:00 p.m. – 4:00 p.m. CT) with a 60-minute break each day beginning at 5:00 p.m. ET (4:00 p.m. CT)
Trading hours	CME ClearPort: 6:00 p.m. Sunday to 6:45 p.m. Friday ET (5:00 p.m. – 5:45 p.m. CT) with a 15-minute maintenance window between 6:45 p.m. – 7:00 p.m. ET (5:45 p.m. – 6:00 p.m. CT) Monday–Thursday.
Product code	Outright: BTC
Listing cycle	Six consecutive monthly contracts inclusive of the nearest two December contracts.

Table 3.
Characteristics of the Bitcoin futures contract. CME.

Contract unit	50 ether
Price quotation	US dollars and cents per ether
	CME Globex: Sunday–Friday 6:00 p.m. – 5:00 p.m. ET (5:00 p.m. – 4:00 p.m. CT) with a 60-minute break each day beginning at 5:00 p.m. ET (4:00 p.m. CT)
Trading hours	CME ClearPort: 6:00 p.m. Sunday to 6:45 p.m. Friday ET (5:00 p.m. – 5:45 p.m. CT) with a 15-minute maintenance window between 6:45 p.m. – 7:00 p.m. ET (5:45 p.m. – 6:00 p.m. CT) Monday–Thursday.
Minimum price fluctuation	Outrights: $0.25 per ether = $12.50 per contract Calendar spreads: $0.05 per ether = $2.50 per contract
Product code	ETH
Listed contracts	Six consecutive monthly contracts inclusive of the nearest two December contracts.
Settlement method	Yes, five contracts minimum
Final settlement day	Last Day of Trading is the last Friday of contract month, Trading in expiring futures terminates at 4:00 p.m. London <?> Day of Trading.
Final settlement price	Delivery is by cash settlement by reference to the final settlement price, equal to the CMECF <?> Reference Rate on the last day of trading.

Table 4.
Characteristics of the futures contract on Ethereum.cme.

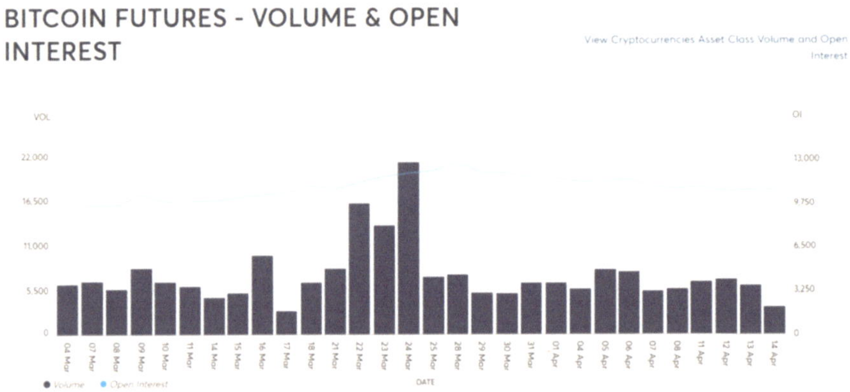

Figure 1.
Open interest and volume of Bitcoin futures contracts.

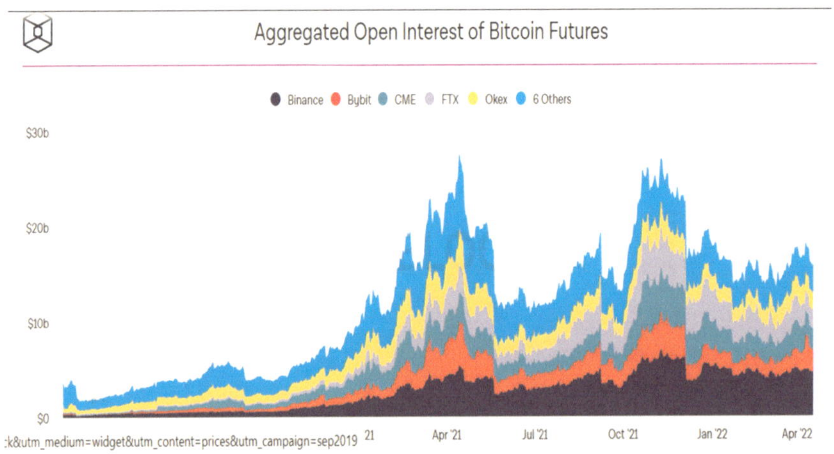

Figure 2.
Open positions on Bitcoin in different instruments. Source: Fireblocks and COINGLASS.

Investment *via* ETFs has several advantages over direct investment, as proposed by Kaushik [3]. As an illustration of these possibilities, **Tables 3** and **4** present the main characteristics of futures contracts on Bitcoin and Ethereum listed on the Chicago Mercantile Exchange (CME).

With regard to the liquidity of operations in Bitcoins, **Figure 1** presents the trading volume and open interest data in futures contracts traded in Chicago.

Many cryptocurrency investors, however, prefer alternative access options to traditional futures, as depicted in **Figure 2**.

As for the correlation with other asset classes and the risk-return trade-off, in the next section, we will conduct a specific analysis of Bitcoin and its effects on its inclusion in investors' portfolios.[2]

[2] In Krückeberg and Scholz [4], a thorough analysis of cryptocurrencies as an asset class is conducted.

2. Introduction to the analysis methodology

The emergence of Bitcoin and other cryptocurrencies and their rapid success as destinations for the investments of hundreds of thousands of investors raises the question of how the inclusion of positions in Bitcoins and other cryptocurrencies influences the risk-return trade-off of a portfolio.

Estimating the profitability of different financial assets in which one can invest is a key consideration in portfolio construction. There are many definitions of the profitability of financial assets, as well as different definitions for each type of asset (fixed income, equities, derivatives, etc.), each with its different valuation methods. Among the more generic and commonly used definitions of the "profitability of a financial asset or security," we highlight the one that states that the profitability of an asset is "the income generated by an investment, expressed as a ratio or percentage."

If we consider the time at which the asset is valued, we can distinguish between:

- *Ex-post or historical return*: this is the return obtained once the transaction is liquidated. This return is known with certainty, as the investment has already been settled. It has no risk because the data is known with certainty. There are multiple academic studies that focus on the analysis of this concept of return for a particular class of assets. In this chapter, we will also analyze the historical returns that investors have obtained with their positions in different cryptocurrencies. Obviously, as stated in financial advertising, past returns do not guarantee future returns. In any case, financial doctrine and practice advise us to study these returns as what seems more stable are the performance differentials between asset classes.

- *Ex-ante or expected return*: this is the estimated return before making the transaction and, therefore, the expected return. The expected return is a random variable that will take different values depending on different scenarios in the future. The statistical measure of the expected return is the mathematical expectation, while the variance and, particularly, the standard deviation will measure the risk borne by the investment.

To determine historical returns, we must set the review period, which we will call "t." In general, the so-called simple return is used as a measure of ex-post return. In this sense, we must reiterate that investors know in advance the return obtained in the past for individual assets. Therefore, the historical return on assets is a magnitude known with certainty.

Generally, the return of asset "i" in the period "t" will be:

$$\mathrm{Ri} = \frac{P_{t+1} - P_t + d_t}{P_t} \tag{1}$$

Where:

R_i = return or yield of asset "i".

P_{t+1} = selling price of asset "i" at the end of the considered period.

P_t = purchase price of security "i".

d_t = intermediate cash flow received from holding the asset (dividends, coupons, etc.). In the case of cryptocurrency investment, this component is zero.

In our analysis of cryptocurrencies, the analysis period will be daily. From daily data, it is trivial to obtain monthly, annual, etc., return data. From these data, we will obtain annualized data for the different assets considered in our analysis to infer the effect of including cryptocurrencies in a portfolio of risky assets.

The other parameter to consider is the risk of assets and portfolios. The most widely used definition by financial markets is that "the risk of an asset is the degree of uncertainty about obtaining the expected return on its financial investments." In this definition, it is considered that risk reflects any variation in this return, whether what we obtain is higher than expected or lower.

There are many ways to assess these potential variations in the return of an asset, with variance being the most commonly used statistical measure. Variance is a measure that expresses the sum of the squares of the deviations of the return of a security from its expected return or its historical return. In our analysis, we will estimate it based on historical data, so we will obtain an estimate of historical volatility.

The most used measure in finance as a risk measure is the standard deviation, which is the square root of the variance and is known in markets as volatility. It is a statistical measure expressed as a percentage and therefore comparable to the other measure we will use, such as return. We refer to this measure as "absolute volatility" because it indicates in absolute value the dispersion of the data that has led to historical returns.[3] If we extend the calculation of these concepts to a portfolio, the return and risk of a combination of assets are obtained by the following formulas:

$$R_p = X_{1p}R_1 + X_{2p}R_2 + \ldots + X_{np}R_n = \Sigma\, X_{ip}R_i \qquad (2)$$

Where:

- R_p = certain return or yield of Portfolio P.
- X_{1p}, X_{2p}, … , X_{np} = percentage distribution of Portfolio P.
- R_1, R_2, … , R_n = certain returns obtained from each security in Portfolio P.

And for risk,

$$\sigma_p^{\,2} = \Sigma\, X_{ip}\, X_{jp}\, \sigma_{ij} = \Sigma\, X_{1p}^{\,2}\, \sigma_i^{\,2} + \Sigma\, X_{ip}\, X_{jp}\, \sigma_{ij} \qquad (3)$$

(For all i different from j)
Where:

- X_{1p}, X_{2p}, …, X_{np} = weight of each asset in Portfolio P.
- σ_{ij} = covariance between the returns of asset i and asset j. Therefore, $\sigma_i^{\,2}$ is the variance of the returns of asset i.

[3] Regarding the risk-return characteristics of Bitcoin, the work of Chaim and Laurini [5] provides valuable insights. Additionally, Chan et al. [6] analyze stochastic distributions that best fit the return series of various cryptocurrencies.

It can be observed that the risk of a portfolio is the sum of the risks of individual assets weighted by their squared weight, plus the sum of the product of the weights of each pair of assets multiplied by their covariance. We know that covariance is equal to:

$$\sigma_{ij} = \sigma_i.\sigma_j.\rho_{ij} \tag{4}$$

Where:
σ_i is the standard deviation of security i
ρ_{ij} is the correlation coefficient between i,j

In this breakdown of the covariance calculation, we see the importance of the correlation between the returns of assets in the diversification of portfolios. This idea already appears in the early works of the Modern Portfolio Theory, initiated by Markowitz [7].[4] In the field of finance professionals, the importance of seeking uncorrelated profitable assets to build portfolios began in the 1970s when knowledge of the Modern Portfolio Theory began to spread. The quest for low correlation explains the trends of:

- Internationally diversifying portfolios since the 1970s.
- Investing in commodities-linked instruments since the 1990s.
- The growing interest of professional investors in "absolute return" investments such as hedge funds since the late 1990s.

As we will explore and analyze, Bitcoin and cryptocurrencies have had a very low or even negative correlation in certain periods with traditional asset classes. This explains why, for many investors guided by quantitative asset management models, this new asset class is very interesting, and they begin to incorporate it into their portfolios.

On the other hand, we should note that most empirical analyses conducted on the effect of including Bitcoin in portfolios use the original version or modified versions of the so-called Markowitz model [7]. Therefore, we believe it is useful to conduct a brief analysis of this model, the cornerstone of Modern Portfolio Theory.

The main contribution of H. Markowitz is to have incorporated into his model the fundamental characteristics of the "rational behavior of the investor," consisting of seeking a portfolio distribution that maximizes returns for a certain level of risk or minimizes risk for a specific return. This process is called the search for efficient portfolios.

The investor has to choose a specific return-risk combination, depending on whether they prefer to achieve more profits by taking on higher risk or by being exposed to lower risk with less profit. The return or yield of the portfolio that an investor expects to obtain in the future is measured, as explained earlier, by the mathematical expectation of the portfolio's return. Risk is measured by the standard deviation or standard deviation of expected returns.

H. Markowitz's model is also known as the Mean-Variance Decision model. In this context, H. Markowitz's fundamental objective was to graphically and analytically

[4] The pioneering work of Markowitz is complemented in his 1958 publication.

demonstrate (linear programming) the relationship between investor expectations (their attitude toward risk) and the choice of an optimal portfolio, always taking into account the two parameters of expected return and risk existing in the market.

The Markowitz model is based on the following assumptions:

1. The return of any asset or portfolio is a subjective random variable, whose probability distribution for the reference period is known by investors. The expected return of the investment is accepted as the measure of the expected return of this random variable.

$$E\left[R_p\right] = X_{1p}\,E[R_1] + X_{2p}\,E[R_2] + \ldots + X_{np}\,E[R_n] = \Sigma\,X_{ip}\,E[R_i] \qquad (5)$$

Where:

- $X_{1p}, X_{2p}, \ldots, X_{np}$ = weight of each asset in Portfolio P.
- $E[R_p], E[R_1]$ .... $E[R_i]$ = expected return of the portfolio, asset 1, asset i

2. The measure of risk is the dispersion of returns, measured by the variance or standard deviation, of the expected return, whether of an individual asset or a portfolio.

$$\sigma_p^2 = \Sigma\,X_{1p}^2\,\sigma_i^2 + \Sigma\,X_{ip}\,X_{jp}\,\sigma_{ij} \qquad (6)$$

Where:

- $X_{1p}, X_{2p}, \ldots, X_{np}$ = Weight of each asset in Portfolio P.
- σ_{ij} = Covariance between the returns of asset i and asset j. Therefore, σ_i^2 is the variance of the returns of asset i.

3. The *investor's utility function* is a function only of the expected return and risk, provided there is rationality in the investor's economic decision-making:

$$U = f\left(E\left[R_p\right], \sigma_p^2\right) \qquad (7)$$

The investor's behavior leads them to prefer portfolios with higher returns and lower risk. Investors prefer to maximize the return on their investment and minimize the risk they must bear. Moreover, as the expected return of the portfolio increases, the utility for the investor increases, and as the risk increases, the utility for the investor decreases.

These three hypotheses or basic assumptions are the basis of H. Markowitz's theory, and they are fulfilled when the probability distribution law followed by the random variable R_p is completely defined by these assumptions or when the investor's utility function is a quadratic function.[5]

---

[5] This theoretical approach is explained in any finance and/or investment management textbook. In my opinion, the analyses conducted in Elton and Gruber [8] chapters 2–4, Bodie et al. [9] chapters 5 and 6, and Francis and Kim [10] chapters 5 and 6 are very illustrative.

Markowitz's goal with his model was to define and obtain the best portfolio or optimal portfolio for each investor. The optimal portfolio is the best one among all that can be formed considering the expected returns of the market and their attitude or aversion to risk. Therefore, the optimal portfolio for one investor may not be optimal for another.

To solve the problem of obtaining efficient portfolios, Markowitz uses a parametric linear optimization model, which can be formulated in two different ways:

(a) For a given value of risk, maximize the expected return:

$$\text{Maximize } E\left[R_p\right] = X_{1p}\,E[R_1] + X_{2p}\,E[R_2] + \ldots + X_{np}\,E[R_n] = \Sigma\, X_{ip}\,E[R_i] \qquad (8)$$

The constraints are:

1. Parametric constraint: the assumed risk

$$\sigma_p^{\,2} = \Sigma\, X_{1p}^{\,2}\,\sigma_i^{\,2} + \Sigma\, X_{ip}\,X_{jp}\,\sigma_{ij} = V^* \qquad (9)$$

where V^* is the value of risk the investor is willing to assume.

2. Investment budget constraint:

$$X_{1p} + X_{2p} + \ldots + X_{np} = 1 \qquad (10)$$

3. Non-negativity condition[6]:

$$X_{1p}; X_{2p}; \ldots; X_{np} \geq 0 \qquad (11)$$

The result for each value of V^* (assumed risk) is a portfolio composition (x_{1p}, x_{2p}, … , x_{np}), which, when substituted into the objective function, provides the maximum expected return for that level of risk. Each assumed level of risk will provide a different portfolio composition (x_{1p}, x_{2p}, … , x_{np}) that is efficient. Thus, the set of efficient portfolios will form the *efficient portfolios frontier*, commonly called the "efficient frontier."

The optimization procedure can be done with a second approach:

(b) Given a certain expected return level, minimize the risk for that return:

$$\text{Minimize } \sigma_p^{\,2} = \Sigma\, X_{1p}^{\,2}\,\sigma_i^{\,2} + \Sigma\, X_{ip}\,X_{jp}\,\sigma_{ij} \qquad (12)$$

The constraints are:

1. Parametric Constraint: The expected return of the portfolio.

$$E\left[R_p\right] = X_{1p}\,E[R_1] + X_{2p}\,E[R_2] + \ldots + X_{np}\,E[R_n] = \Sigma\, X_{ip}\,E[R_i] = E^* \qquad (13)$$

---

[6] In modern applications of the Markowitz model, the budget constraint and the non-negativity constraint on weights are sometimes not considered due to the possibilities of taking "short" positions in assets and the leverage that can be achieved using derivatives, for example.

Where E* is the expected return the investor wants to achieve, and thus the optimization problem must be solved with it.

2. Investment budget constraint

$$X_{1p} + X_{2p} + \ldots + X_{np} = 1 \tag{14}$$

3. Non-negativity condition

$$X_{1p}; X_{2p}; \ldots ; X_{np} \geq 0 \tag{15}$$

The result for each value of E* is a portfolio composition (X_{1p}+ X_{2p}+ … + X_{np}), which, when substituted into the objective function, provides the minimum risk of the portfolio for that specific level of return. The set of efficient portfolios will form the efficient frontier.

A portfolio is said to be efficient if there is no other portfolio that provides a higher return for the same level of risk or that provides a lower risk for the same return. Such portfolios are graphically located at the upper end of the possible portfolio space so that the set of all efficient portfolios forms a curve commonly called the "efficient frontier." The efficient frontier has a parabolic shape, as seen in **Figure 3**.

The analysis of the positive effects that cryptocurrencies, such as Bitcoin, can have on investors' portfolios must objectively determine, based on optimization models, whether this asset class should be present in the composition of efficient portfolios. As we will discuss, this has already been investigated by various authors who generally conclude that cryptocurrencies improve (shift upward and to the left) the efficient frontier for investors.

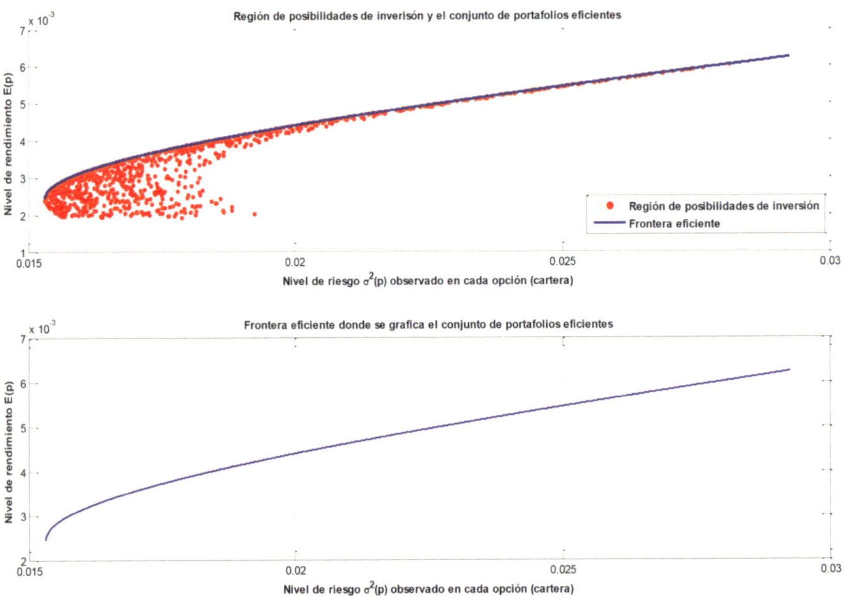

Figure 3.
Graphical representation of the efficient frontier in portfolio analysis.

3. Analyses have been conducted on the diversification effects in Bitcoin and cryptocurrency portfolios

In Gangwal [11], one of the initial analyses of the positive effects of introducing Bitcoin into portfolios[7] is found, conducted at a simple and introductory level. One of the most comprehensive pioneering studies on the effects of including Bitcoin in a portfolio of financial assets was conducted by Katjazi and Moro [13], using monthly data from January 31, 2012, to January 31, 2017. The asset classes used in the analysis are listed in **Table 5**. The selected asset classes include gold, equities, fixed income, money markets, commodities, real estate, and even alternative investments through a hedge fund index. These authors approach the analysis of the effect of including Bitcoin from the perspective of an investor based in the USA, the eurozone, or China.

	Name	Mnemonic	Asset class
United States	BTC-USD-Index	billus	Cryptocurrency
	S&P U.S. TREASURY BILL INDEX	billus	Money Market
	S&P U.S. TREASURY BOND INDEX	condus	Fixed-income
	DOW JONES EQUAL WEIGHTS U.S. ISSUED CORPORATE BONDS	corpus	Fixed-income
	S&P WCI GOLD (ER)	gold	Gold ETF
	S&P 100	sp100	Equity (large cap)
	S&P 500	sp500	Equity (mid cap)
	S&P 600	spsml	Equity (small cap)
	S&P WCI	wcig	Commodities
	DOW JONES U.S. REAL EASTATE INDEX	resus	Real Estate
	Global hedge fund index	hfrx	Alternative
	Dow Jones FXCM Dollar Index	usdollar	Currency
Europe	BTC	btceur	Cryptocurrency
	S&P Pan-Europe Developed Sovereign Bond Index	condeu	Fixed-income
	S&P Eurozone Investment Grade Corporate Bond Index	corpeu	Fixed-income
	S&P WCI GOLD (ER)	gold	Gold ETF
	S&P EUROPE 350	sp350eu	Equity
	S&P WCI Europe	wcie	Commodities
	Dow Jones Europe Select Real Estate Securities Index	reseu	Real Estate
	Global hedge fund index	hfrx	Alternative
	S&P EURO Futures Index Spot	speuf	Currency

[7] In Gasser et al. [12], one can find one of the first analyses of this issue. The problem is that at the time of conducting the analysis, there were few data available, and the first months of Bitcoin's operation are included, which may distort the results.

	Name	Mnemonic	Asset class
China	BTC-CNY-Index	btccny	Cryptocurrency
	S&P CHINA GOVERNMENT BILL INDEX	billcn	Money Market
	S&P CHINA SOVEREIGN BOND INDEX	condcn	Fixed-income
	S&P CHINA CORPORATE BOND INDEX	corpcn	Fixed-income
	S&P WCI GOLD (ER)	gold	Gold ETF
	S&P CHINA A 100 INDEX (RMB)	spc100	Equity (large cap)
	S&P CHINA A 200 INDEX (RMB)	spc200	Equity (mid cap)
	S&P CHINA A SMALLCAP INDEX (RMB)	spcsml	Equity (small cap)
	S&P WCI ASIA	wcia	Commodities
	Guggenheim China Real Estate ETF (TAO)	tao	Real Estate
	Global hedge fund index	hfrx	Alternative
	USDCNY Exchange rate (holding USD as investment)	usdcny	Currency

Source: Katjazi and Moro [13].

Table 5.
Asset classes used in the study by Katjazi and Moro.

Additionally, they propose four optimization scenarios using the Markowitz approach discussed earlier:

1. Equitably distributing the portfolio among the various possible asset classes. This alternative does not aim to identify an optimal investment portfolio but to verify whether, in the case of Bitcoin, what was stated by Demiguel et al. [14] holds true—that an equally weighted portfolio behaves similarly to an optimized portfolio in terms of mean-variance, using the well-known Sharpe performance ratio. This ratio, developed by Nobel laureate economist Sharpe [15], is defined by the expression:

$$S = \frac{R - R_f}{\sigma} \tag{16}$$

   Where:

   - S: is the Sharpe ratio.
   - R: is the portfolio/asset return to be analyzed.
   - R_f: is the risk-free asset return.
   - σ is the standard deviation of portfolio returns.

2. All weights in the portfolio are positive, meaning no short positions are allowed in any asset class.

3. Short positions are allowed without leverage, meaning all weights w_i must be between −1 and 1, and the sum must equal unity. In this case, the possibility of leverage on assets is restricted.

4. Short positions are allowed with the rule of the previous alternative, except for Bitcoin, which cannot be included as a short position.

For the three economic areas considered in the analysis, Bitcoin appears as the most profitable asset class. Additionally, they propose an analysis where the portfolio is reviewed monthly to dynamically analyze the effect of Bitcoin on portfolios. In **Table 6**, we present, for simplicity, only the results for the European investor. It can be verified that, in an optimized portfolio, particularly in portfolios without leverage and without short positions, Bitcoin becomes a relevant asset for Eurozone investors.

Although there are a couple of months where the optimized portfolio takes short positions in Bitcoins, in general, a positive exposure is always adopted. The conclusions of the analysis are as follows [13]:

1. The inclusion of Bitcoin improves the profitability of portfolios in most cases.

2. Only in some cases of optimization from the perspective of U.S. and Chinese investors does the inclusion of Bitcoin worsen the profitability of portfolios. According to these authors, this happens in 3 out of the 21 scenarios analyzed.

Subsequently, Bakry et al. [16] conducted a very interesting analysis from the perspective of an American investor, using variables similar to those in the study by Katjazi and Moro [13] and adding others such as the Baltic Exchange Dry Index (BDI), considered a good indicator of real economic activity, and an index linked to the energy sector, DJUBENS (Dow Jones-UBS Energy Spot Subindex). The time period used to build the database was from August 2011 to May 2021 with weekly observations, which means using 508 observations for each variable.

Semi-annual BTC weights			
Portfolio	**Long-only (%)**	**Semi-C. (%)**	**btc > l (%)**
Jun-13	35.46	11.52	11.52
Dec-13	17.53	6.82	6.82
Jun-14	16.25	1.39	1.39
Dec-14	0.28	0.01	0.01
Jun-15	0.00	−2.02	0.00
Dec-15	55.05	−2.37	0.00
Jun-16	26.15	1.26	1.26
Dec-16	56.31	1.71	1.71
Bitcoin mean	25.88	2.29	2.84

Source: Katjazi and Moro [13].

Table 6.
Dynamic inclusion of Bitcoin in the portfolio of a European Investor.

Their analysis approach starts with the typical mean-variance optimizer proposed by Markowitz [7], using the Sharpe ratio as the variable to maximize. The conclusion these authors reach is that Bitcoin represents an asset class with a positive diversification effect in portfolios. This is because the risk-return or performance[8] combination of portfolios that include this cryptocurrency is better than that obtained with portfolios without the cryptocurrency.

Additionally, the study by Kim [17] also confirms the positive effects of including cryptocurrencies in investor portfolios.

Finally, we must refer to the study by Liu [18], which analyzes the characteristics for investors of portfolios composed only of cryptocurrencies. Obviously, it does not make sense for an investor to only invest in crypto-assets, but analyzing the diversification effects within this investment universe is useful. The data used in the study includes daily prices from August 7, 2015, to August 8, 2018.

In **Figure 4**, we present the correlation matrix between the returns of the cryptocurrencies included in the analysis. Interestingly, the correlations are not very high, so if this characteristic holds over time, the diversification benefits among cryptocurrencies will be notable.

Based on these data and those related to the performance and volatility of the different cryptocurrencies analyzed, Liu [18] constructs an efficient frontier for this asset class, which we reproduce for its interest in **Figure 5**.

As observed in **Figure 5**, neither Bitcoin nor Ethereum is on the efficient frontier, implying that there are theoretical potential benefits for investors who explore the possibilities of other cryptocurrencies present in the market.

It is also true that expanding the range of investment assets to lesser-known cryptocurrencies dramatically increases the risk of fraud, operational risks, liquidity

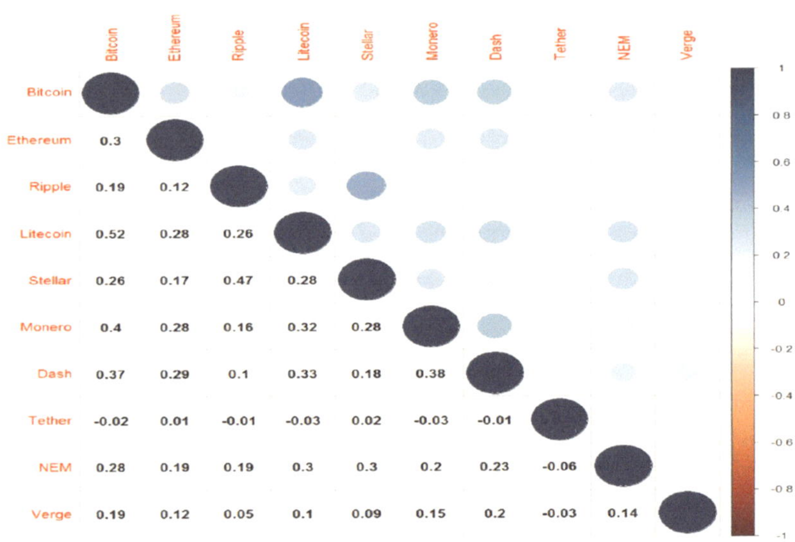

Figure 4.
Correlations between cryptocurrency returns. Source: Liu [18], p. 202.

[8] In the language of portfolio management, performance is the measure of risk-adjusted return that allows us to compare portfolios exposed to different levels of volatility. See Bodie et al. [9], chap. 20.

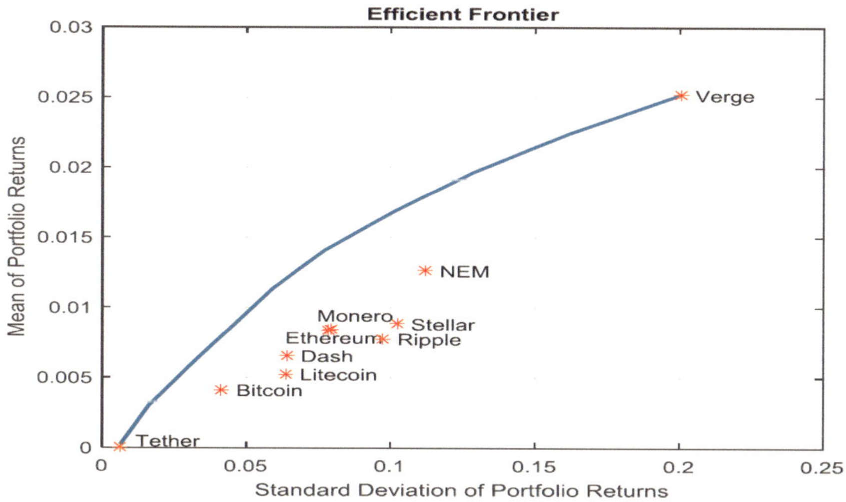

Figure 5.
Efficient cryptocurrency frontier. Source: Liu [18], p. 203.

risk, etc., issues that cannot be adequately captured by quantitative portfolio optimization models.

On the other hand, Lotho et al. [19] analyze the effects of including crypto assets in a portfolio of a South African investor, an example of an investor based in an emerging market. The results are spectacular, as shown in **Figure 6**.

The blue line represents the efficient frontier using traditional asset classes and alternative investments except for cryptocurrencies. The red line shows the efficient frontier when considering the possibility of investing in cryptocurrencies through the CRIX index. This index is calculated in real-time by the Chair of Statistics Ladislaus von Bortkiewicz at Humboldt University, Berlin, Germany, supported for this purpose by professors from Singapore Management University. The index is composed of the 10 most relevant cryptocurrencies.

There is no doubt that the positive results in terms of risk-return performance from including crypto assets in portfolios are remarkable in all analyzed studies. An important question that we will later examine is whether these results can be sustained over time.

4. Empirical analysis from the perspective of a European investor

To test the hypothesis that Bitcoin, Ethereum, and, by extension, other cryptocurrencies have positive effects on the risk-return profile of financial asset portfolios for European investors, we conducted an empirical study based on the following methodology and databases.

Regarding the data, we considered daily observations of the following indices and prices from July 18, 2010, to December 31, 2021, for Bitcoin and from January 18, 2018, to December 31, 2021, for Ethereum.

To represent other risky asset classes, we selected the following indices:

- Future price of gold on CME expressed in dollars.

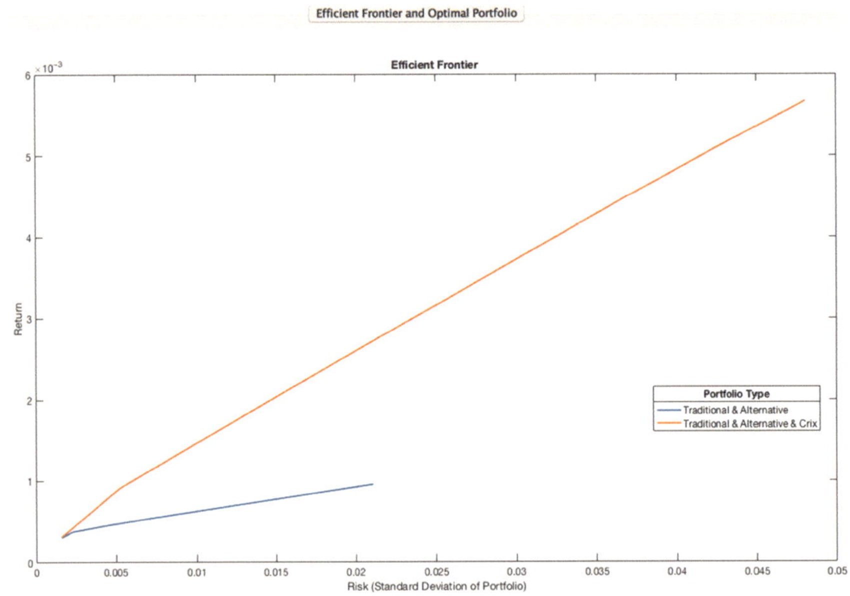

Figure 6.
Effects of including crypto assets for a South African investor. Source: Lotho et al. [19].

- Bitcoin price expressed in dollars according to the COINBASE platform.
- Ethereum price expressed in dollars according to the BIBOX platform.
- Standard & Poor's 500 index from the U.S. stock market.
- EUROSTOXX 50 index from the European stock market.
- EONIA interest rate index for day-to-day money market operations in euros. It is a proxy for the risk-free interest rate for European investors.
- Day-to-day interest rate index for the U.S. dollar.
- Dollar/euro exchange rate.

We obtained data for stock market indices, gold futures, and cryptocurrency prices from the INVESTING.COM portal. The interest rate and exchange rate data come from the BLOOMBERG database.

The performance data of the two cryptocurrencies against other risky assets provide a profile of much more profitable assets, although, as we will see later, with very high risk (**Table 7**).

The level of risk is measured through the standard deviation of the daily returns of different assets, subsequently annualized. The data obtained for this variable for the last two years are presented in **Table 8**.

It is evident that the high returns of cryptocurrencies were achieved at the cost of assuming high volatility. To complete this descriptive analysis, we have estimated the

Fecha	Gold (%)	S&P (%)	EuroStoxx50 (%)	Bitcoin (%)	ETH (%)	Eonia Index (%)	USD 1D Index (%)	USDEUR (%)
1 YEAR	−4,471	25,054	20,992	55,577	372,418	−0,007	−0,001	−6,837
2 YEARS	16,803	48,236	14,773	550,385	2787,572	−0,060	−1,504	1,499
5 YEARS	48,319	122,140	30,630	5106,415	-.-	−0,178	−0,640	8,197

Table 7.
Performance in Euros of the analyzed assets.

	Volatility 2021 (%)	Volatility 2020–2021 (%)
Gold	15,038	19,017
S&P	13,067	26,115
EuroStoxx50	15,076	25,206
Bitcoin	77,098	73,477
ETH	97,587	92,881
Eonia Index	0,061	0,056
USD 1D Index	0,511	1,054
USDEUR	5,831	6,759

Table 8.
Volatility data of analyzed assets.

Sharpe ratio of the risky assets considered in our analysis, taking the EONIA return as the risk-free return. To avoid favoring cryptocurrencies, we exclusively used data from 2021. The data is presented in **Table 9**.

To complete the analysis, we also estimated for each asset class from the beginning of Bitcoin on July 18, 2010, until December 31, 2021, except for Ethereum, whose data starts on January 18, 2018. Based on this widely used ratio in the markets, it is clear that cryptocurrencies present a great appeal in terms of the risk-return trade-off they offer for any European investor. It is noteworthy that, among the chosen asset portfolio, Bitcoin is the most attractive from its appearance date.

Moreover, it is crucial to understand the correlations between the returns of risky assets and cryptocurrencies to decide on the portfolio composition.

In **Table 10**, we present these correlations for the year 2021 and the period 2021–2022.

	Sharpe Ratio 2021	Historical profitability (%)	Historical Vol (%)	Historical sharpe Ratio
Gold	−0,24	4,20	24,00	0,17
S&P	0,96	12,72	17,16	0,74
EuroStoxx50	0,83	2,99	20,50	0,15
Bitcoin	0,76	196,53	131,96	**1,49**
ETH	4,01	38,66	83,42	0,46

Table 9.
Sharpe ratio for the European investor of different asset classes.

Correlations 1 Year	**Gold (%)**	**S&P (%)**	**EuroStoxx50 (%)**	**Bitcoin (%)**	**ETH (%)**	**Eonia Index (%)**	**USD 1D Index (%)**	**USDEUR (%)**
Gold	100,000	5,335	4,335	−6,120	3,611	3,474	12,241	36,688
S&P	5,335	100,000	52,503	30,177	27,641	2,693	4,636	17,489
EuroStoxx50	4,335	52,503	100,000	24,356	26,394	10,707	4,693	2,886
Bitcoin	−6,120	30,177	24,356	100,000	78,579	2,925	−3,996	8,184
ETH	3,611	27,641	26,394	78,579	100,000	10,419	−6,284	15,808
Eonia Index	3,474	2,693	10,707	2,925	10,419	100,000	6,154	9,272
USD 1D Index	12,241	4,636	4,693	−3,996	−6,284	6,154	100,000	−0,355
USDEUR	36,688	17,489	2,886	8,184	15,808	9,272	−0,355	100,000
Correlations 2 Years	Gold (%)	S&P (%)	EuroStoxx50 (%)	Bitcoin (%)	ETH (%)	Eonia Index (%)	USD 1D Index (%)	USDEUR (%)
Gold	100,000	14,625	11,731	12,775	14,199	−2,489	13,160	27,749
S&P	14,625	100,000	65,693	33,584	34,576	−4,024	13,294	1,889
EuroStoxx50	11,731	65,693	100,000	29,534	27,923	3,708	10,298	2,616
Bitcoin	12,775	33,584	29,534	100,000	81,966	0,042	−2,638	5,713
ETH	14,199	34,576	27,923	81,966	100,000	4,510	−2,138	8,638
Eonia Index	−2,489	−4,024	3,708	0,042	4,510	100,000	0,680	5,201
USD 1D Index	13,160	13,294	10,298	−2,638	−2,138	0,680	100,000	7,066
USDEUR	27,749	1,889	2,616	5,713	8,638	5,201	7,066	100,000

Table 10.
Correlations between analyzed asset classes.

A relevant question is the timeperiod to consider for estimating correlations. In this case, the furthest initial date should be taken as July 2015, as Ethereum was introduced in that month. Additionally, in the early years of cryptocurrency operation, factors could bias their correlation downward and obviously alter their return and risk parameters. These factors include:

- Investors' lack of awareness of the investment attractiveness of cryptocurrencies.

- Lack of liquidity in cryptocurrencies.

- The initial segmentation of the cryptocurrency market to investors and economic agents seeking fiscal and financial "opacity," etc.

These factors likely alter the distribution of returns of these assets. From 2020 onwards, we can consider that well-known cryptocurrencies such as Bitcoin and Ethereum are integrated into the universe of potential investment assets for millions of investors worldwide, and their returns should be more representative of possible future behavior than returns from previous years.

In any case, we have studied the evolution of the correlation between Bitcoin and stock market assets based on different analyzed studies. In **Figure 7**, we represent the evolution of the correlation between the price of Bitcoin in US dollars and the SP500 index.

Regarding the relationship between Euro-denominated Bitcoin returns and European equities, the correlation increases from the value obtained of 0,145 in the study by Katjazi and Moro [13] to the value of 0,295 in **Table 10**. A significant increase in Bitcoin correlation over the last two years can be observed compared to the analysis of a more extended period. This is logical as Bitcoin becomes more integrated with the rest of the financial asset markets. Regardless of the comments we will make later on the future of cryptocurrencies as an asset class, investors should assume the hypothesis of an increase in future Bitcoin correlation with equities as crypto assets become more integrated with publicly traded stocks.

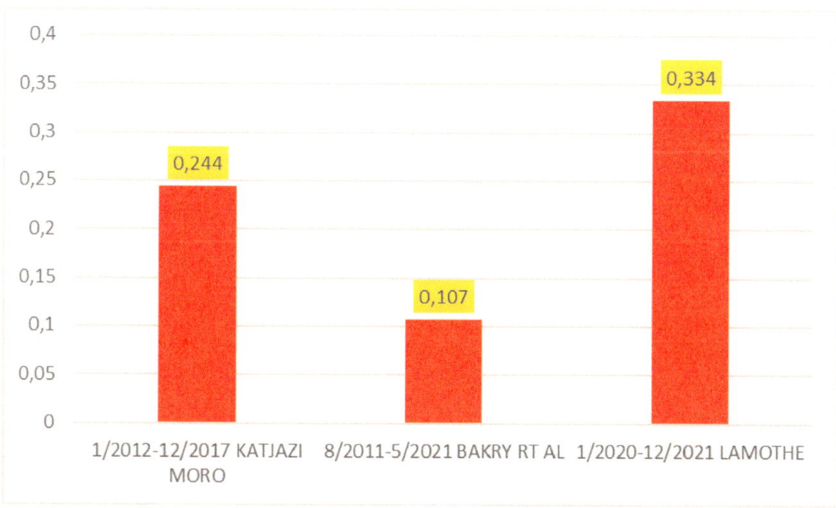

Figure 7.
Evolution of the correlation between Bitcoin and the SP 500 Index.

	PROFITABILITY (%)	RISK (%)
DIVERSIFICATION NAIF	31,65	23,17
OPTIMA RATIO SHARPE	47,46	17,74
MIN VARIANCE	−0,10	0,58
MIN VARIANCE 5%	5,00	1,87
MIN VARIANCE 10%	10,00	3,74
MIN VARIANCE 20%	20,00	7,48
MIN VARIANCE 30%	30,00	11,21
MIN VARIANCE 40%	40,00	14,95

Table 11.
Performance and risk of optimized portfolios.

With the mentioned data, we conducted different portfolio optimization exercises. Specifically, we constructed the following portfolios:

- A portfolio with "naive" diversification, equally weighting different asset classes.
- Minimum variance portfolios for different levels of return without short positions.
- The portfolio that allows obtaining the maximum Sharpe ratio.

We did not consider portfolios with short positions as they are not the usual strategy for common investors.

The results in terms of returns and risks for the optimized portfolios are shown in **Table 11**. The return is expressed in updated terms, and the risk is the updated standard deviation of that return.

What is very interesting is the analysis of the portfolio composition. These portfolios always consist of positions in low-risk assets (money markets in euros and dollars) with positions in Bitcoin, as shown in **Table 12**.

ASSET	NAIF (%)	MIN VAR (%)	MIN VAR 10% (%)	MIN VAR 20% (%)	MIN VAR 30% (%)	MIN VAR 40% (%)	SHARPE (%)
Gold	12,50	0,00	0,00	0,00	0,00	0,00	0,00
S&P	12,50	0,00	0,00	0,00	0,00	0,00	0,00
EuroStoxx50	12,50	0,00	0,00	0,00	0,00	0,00	0,00
Bitcoin	12,50	0,03	5,09	10,18	15,26	20,35	24,15
ETH	12,50	0,00	0,00	0,00	0,00	0,00	0,00
Eonia Index	12,50	39,22	85,31	70,86	56,41	41,96	31,05
USD 1D Index	12,50	52,76	9,61	18,97	28,33	37,68	44,80
USDEUR	12,50	7,99	0,00	0,00	0,00	0,00	0,00
	100,00	100,00	100,00	100,00	100,00	100,00	100,00

Table 12.
Composition of optimized portfolios.

Even the minimum variance portfolio has a slight position in Bitcoins. In other words, given the excellent performance of Bitcoin in the two years analyzed, investors would use it as the risky asset to include in their portfolios. Conventional risky assets, such as equity assets, would not be of interest to investors.

Our results align with those obtained in other empirical analyses. For example, in the study by Katjazi and Moro [13] for European investors with portfolios without short positions, the average Bitcoin investment is 25.88% for the period June 2013 to December 2016. Interestingly, this position is less relevant for investors with the dollar as the base currency, as the average weight of Bitcoin in portfolios only reaches 5.47% for the same period.[9]

Empirical data are decisive regarding the appeal of Bitcoin and, by extension, other cryptocurrencies as an asset class. The significant question is whether this appeal is merely circumstantial and will eventually fade, making investors less concerned about this new asset class. In the next section, we will try to address, at least partially, these questions.

5. Can the appeal of cryptocurrencies be considered structural?

Doubts arise regarding the excellent performance of Bitcoin and other cryptocurrencies as an asset class based on two analytical approaches.

The first assumes that Bitcoin and crypto assets are nothing more than another episode of speculative bubbles in the market, akin to the tulip bulb mania in the seventeenth century.

The second approach links Bitcoin and cryptocurrency return to the outstanding performance of so-called technology stocks. This perspective suggests that investing in Bitcoins is a variant of investing in technology.

6. Is Bitcoin a new episode of speculative bubble?

As observed in **Figure 8**, some authors compare what happened with Bitcoin in recent years with the historical evolution of other assets that generated "price bubbles." **Figure 8**, taken from The Economist magazine, is a good example of the hypothesis that Bitcoin was experiencing the formation and subsequent bursting of a new speculative bubble in 2017. The truth is that the bubble burst predicted by the chart for 2017 did not occur at all. Four years later, Bitcoin multiplied its price several times compared to the 2017 level.

Indeed, there are several academic works that insist on the idea that Bitcoin and other cryptocurrencies are just another variant of speculative bubbles in market history.

Chea and Fry [20], in one of the earliest academic analyses of Bitcoin,[10] concluded that:

- Bitcoin and other cryptocurrencies are assets prone to experiencing price bubbles.

[9] For Chinese investors, the weight would also be lower by 7.17%.

[10] The idea that there was a speculative bubble in Bitcoin is already present in Dowd [21].

- The "bubble" content within the price of Bitcoin is very high.
- The fundamental value of Bitcoin is zero.

Professional cryptocurrency specialists such as Parker [22] modeled the phases of a bubble burst, as shown in **Figure 9**, following the model by Rodrigue et al. [23], which has become the paradigm for explaining the evolution of bubbles.[11]

It is challenging to fit the evolution of Bitcoin into the bubble model proposed by Rodrigue et al. [23] for any speculative asset. For example, in Rodrigue's model, institutional investment begins acquiring the speculative asset before the general public does. As mentioned earlier, institutional investors in developed markets have started showing interest in Bitcoin after hundreds of thousands of individual investors have already invested in crypto assets. Cryptocurrencies have experienced a significant price adjustment this year due to solvency issues with "stablecoins" like TERRA LUNA, but as of the time of writing, they are in a recovery phase.

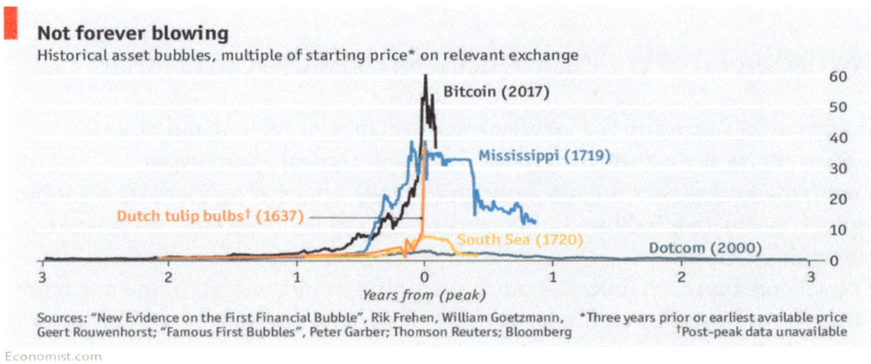

Figure 8.
Bitcoin vs. other speculative bubbles. Source: The Economist, Abril 2017.

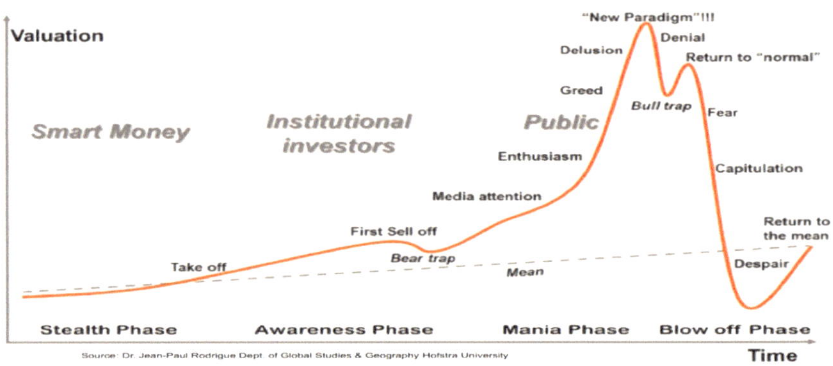

Figure 9.
Evolution model of a price bubble by Rodrigue et al. [23]. Source: Rodrigue et al. [23].

[11] Jean Paul Rodrigue, a professor of economic geography, provided a graphical explanation that went "viral." It was published around February 2008 in a non-conventional format. See https://commons.wikimedia.org/wiki/File:Stages_of_a_bubble.png

It is true that the cryptocurrency market is susceptible to various scams, pyramid schemes, and other fraudulent activities targeting investors. However, this is not the case for "serious" cryptocurrencies like Bitcoin and Ethereum.

Regarding the fundamental value of Bitcoin, Podhorsky [24] developed a micro-economic model of Bitcoin production to estimate it.

The model established that the fundamental value of a Bitcoin is equal to the equipment and electricity costs of miners in relation to their expected block reward. This idea of the fundamental value of Bitcoin associated with its mining cost is also presented in Hayes [25].

The association between the fundamental value of Bitcoin and its production cost is also behind the popular ratio or coefficient MVRV used by cryptocurrency specialists. This ratio was proposed by Mahmudov and Puell [26] and is widely used in the fundamental analysis of cryptocurrencies.

The MVRV ratio is the quotient between the capitalization of a cryptocurrency and the cost incurred for the "mining" or obtaining of its current volume. In other words, the ratio is equal to MV/RV, where:

- MV = market value. Unit price multiplied by the number of circulating cryptocurrencies. For example, for Bitcoin, it's the circulating Bitcoins multiplied by their price.
- RV = realized value. Cost of extraction, mining, and/or obtaining of all existing cryptocurrencies at the time of calculation. For Bitcoin, it would be the amount paid for all circulating Bitcoins. This can be calculated by analyzing data on the Bitcoin blockchain. It involves tracking when Bitcoins were last moved from one wallet to another and calculating the price at that moment. Then, all these obtaining costs are added up to reach the total realized value.[12]

Obviously, this ratio is calculated for a particular cryptocurrency, and its value gives an idea of whether the price deviates from its production cost. In **Figure 10**, the evolution of this ratio is shown according to the financial services company AK INVESTMENT MANAGEMENT LLC (2021).

According to Elmandjra and Puell [28],[13] "historically, the price of Bitcoin has had a 'ceiling' when the ratio has exceeded a value of 10." It seems as if there is a mean-reversion process for the ratio, which, according to their analysis, would settle at a value of 3.

In this line of analysis, it is also interesting to explore whether "herding behavior" occurs in Bitcoin or not. Herding behaviors occur when, generally in times of high market volatility, investors follow the decisions of the majority of the market without adequately analyzing what is most suitable for their objectives and needs. In the financial markets, these behaviors translate into buying when the majority of investors buy or selling when the majority sells, without relying on specific analysis or relevant evidence.

Obviously, these herd effects fuel the creation of speculative bubbles, and when investors adopt a pessimistic view, they accelerate the "bursting" of bubbles.[14] This has happened in other speculative markets, as shown, for example, in Thoma [30].

---

[12] The value of this ratio can be easily obtained on various websites specializing in cryptocurrencies.

[13] Elmandjra and Puell [28], p. 20.

[14] The relationship between bubbles and herd behavior can be found in the already classic work by Brunnermeier [29].

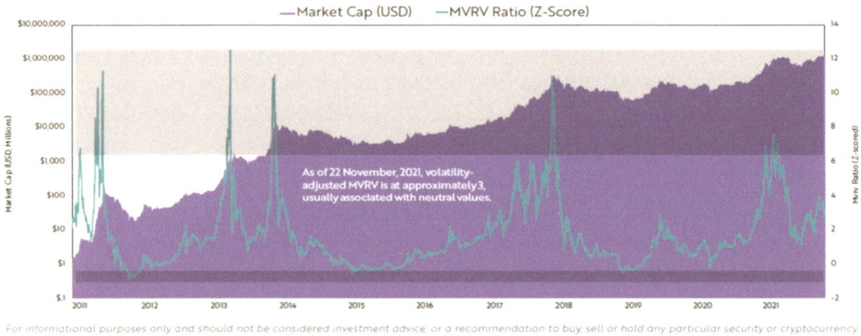

Figure 10.
MVRV ratio evolution. Source: ARK INVESTMENT MANAGEMENT LLC [27].

Bouri et al. [31] conducted an interesting study on this issue for 14 cryptocurrencies, representing 68.36% of the market, in the period from April 28, 2013, to May 2, 2018. Their analysis followed the methodology of Chang et al. [32], using the Cross Section Standard Absolute Deviation (CSAD) or Cross Section Standard Absolute Deviation as a proxy for the dispersion of asset returns and the asset return as a test for herding behaviors.

Herding behaviors generally occur in periods of market stress and strong price movements. In that context, the relationship between returns and their dispersion is non-linear. Bouri et al. [31] show that the cryptocurrency market is subject to herding behaviors that seem to vary over time. The high degree of correlation in the returns of different cryptocurrencies implies that cryptocurrency investors imitate the investment decisions of others.
According to these authors, evidence of herding behavior suggests insufficient portfolio diversification, exposing investors who only hold cryptocurrencies to additional risk.

Poyser-Calderon [33] conducted a similar study for the top 100 cryptocurrencies in the COINMARKET database for the same period as the previous authors. The results are similar to the earlier analysis, with the author concluding that investors often deviated from the rational asset price analysis model and chose to follow consensus in market stress situations.

On the other hand, Jalan et al. [34] verify the generation of bubbles in different stocks in recent years, including those issued by listed companies linked to the world of cryptocurrencies.

7. Are cryptocurrencies an investment alternative to tech stocks?

In **Figure 11**, we present an interesting graph compiled by the investment bank Credit Suisse in 2021, showing the apparent high correlation between the price of Bitcoin in US dollars and the so-called FANG index or FAANG, composed of the stocks of the five major American technology companies: Facebook, Amazon, Netflix, Google, and the latest addition, Apple. This index was created by the New York Stock Exchange and includes the five major technology companies listed on the Nasdaq. What started as a term coined to encompass the most important American technology

Figure 11.
Correlation between Bitcoin price and FAANG Index. Source: Credit Suisse (2021).

companies has ultimately become a valid reference index to verify what happens with major technology companies in the stock markets.[15]

Although the evolution until 2021 has been very similar for Bitcoin and major tech stocks, there are nuances worth highlighting that do not allow including cryptocurrencies in a generic tech asset class. For example, Vidal [36] conducted an interesting study for the triennium 2017–2019 on the risk-adjusted profitability of major cryptocurrencies compared to the stocks of the most important American tech companies, components of the FAANG index. As seen in **Figures 12** and **13**, the three analyzed cryptocurrencies—Bitcoin, Ether, and Ripple (XRP)—have a risk-adjusted return worse than tech stocks. The Sharpe ratios are 0.84 for Ether, 0.81 for Bitcoin, and 0.75 for Ripple. For tech stocks, they presented Sharpe ratios of 1.59 (APPLE), 1.33 (AMAZON), 1.04 (NETFLIX), 0.95 (GOOGLE), and 0.76 (FACEBOOK). Except for the last stock, the risk-adjusted performance of

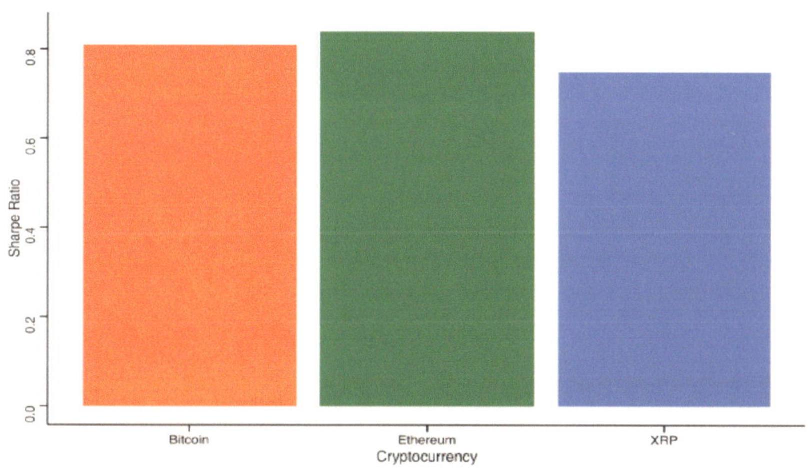

Figure 12.
Sharpe ratio for cryptocurrency investment 2017–2019. Source: Vidal [36].

[15] Some authors have suggested the existence of a bubble also in technology stocks. See Özduraka and Karataş [35].

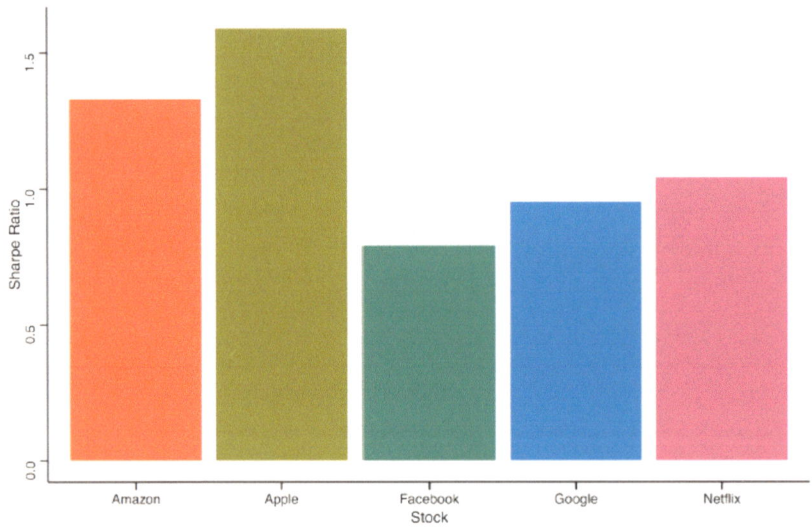

Figure 13.
Sharpe ratio for FAANG Investment 2017–2019. Source: Vidal [36].

tech stocks was better than that of cryptocurrencies, despite the high returns of cryptocurrencies during the analyzed period.

To study this question, we conducted a comparative analysis between Bitcoin and the FAANG index for the period from September 30, 2017, to August 20, 2022, i.e., the last four years based on INVESTING data. The evolution of both assets, with their quotation set at 100 on September 30, 2017, is shown in **Figure 14**.

We can observe how Bitcoin experiences an explosive bullish trend starting from November 2020, which does not occur with the same intensity in the FAANG index. In contrast, from November 2021, Bitcoin undergoes a significant correction until August 2022, amounting to 64.81% from its peak, while the FAANG index only corrects by 27.87% from its highs. Regarding the correlation between both assets, it is only 0.257 based on monthly return data, making it difficult to assume that they belong to the same asset class.

Figure 14.
Bitcoin vs. FAANG evolution 2017 (Sep)–2022 (Aug).

Finally, concerning the Sharpe ratio, during the period, Bitcoin provided a ratio of 0.235 based on monthly data, while the FAANG index provided a ratio of 0.264 also based on monthly data. In other words, technological stocks continue to provide a higher risk-adjusted return than Bitcoin.

Therefore, empirical evidence allows us to make two conclusions:

1. Investment in cryptocurrencies, especially Bitcoin, has improved the risk-return trade-off for investors in recent years. However, it cannot be asserted that this positive effect will persist in the future as the correlation between Bitcoin and other similar assets increases with conventional investments, and their returns "normalize." In fact, Nguyen [37] demonstrates that during periods of higher uncertainty, such as during COVID-19, the correlation between Bitcoin's performance and the performance of the S&P 500 index increased significantly.

2. Bitcoin and cryptocurrencies are not components of the "Tech Stocks" asset class. While they have had similar behavior in some periods, the volatility of cryptocurrencies is much higher than that of tech stocks.

Another interesting aspect of Bitcoin investment, according to Kim [38], is that it is more beneficial to invest in spot positions in Bitcoin than through futures contracts. In their analysis based on Bitcoin futures market quotes from CME between December 2017 and December 2019, spot positions had an average performance premium of 5.4% compared to futures positions. This differential is explained by the difficulty of taking "short" positions in the Bitcoin spot market, preventing arbitrage.

Clearly, the emergence of new empirical evidence on Bitcoin and cryptocurrencies will allow us to confirm these ideas and more precisely assess the effect of their introduction into investors' portfolios.

Author details

Prosper Lamothe-López[1]*, Prosper Lamothe-Fernández[2]
and Leslie Rodríguez-Valencia[3]

1 Department of Business Economics, Universidad Rey Juan Carlos, Madrid, Spain

2 Department of Finance and Commercial Research, Universidad Autónoma de Madrid, Madrid, Spain

3 Department of Economy and Business, Universidad Europea de Madrid, Madrid, Spain

*Address all correspondence to: prosper.lamothe@uam.es

References

[1] Greer RJ. What is an asset class, anyway? Journal of Portfolio Management. 1997;**23**:86-91

[2] Burniske C, White A. Bitcoin: Ringing the Bell to a New Asset Class. New York: ARK INVEST Research; 2016. pp. 1-25. Available from: https://research.ark-invest.com/hubfs/1_Download_Files_ARK-Invest/White_Papers/Bitcoin-Ringing-The-Bell-For-A-New-Asset-Class.pdf

[3] Kaushik P. Bitcoin ETFs: What they are and how to invest (in 2022). Bitcoin Market Journal. 2021. Available from: https://www.bitcoinmarketjournal.com/bitcoin-etf/

[4] Krückeberg S, Scholz P. Cryptocurrencies as an asset class? In: Gouette S, Khaled G, Saadi S, editors. Cryptofinance and Mechanisms of Exchange – The Making of Virtual Currency. Springer International Publishing; 2019. pp. 1-28. DOI: 10.1007/978-3-030-30738-7

[5] Chaim P, Laurini MP. Volatility and return jumps in Bitcoin. Economics Letters. 2018;**173**:158-163

[6] Chan S, Chu J, Nadarajah S, Osterrieder J. A statistical analysis of cryptocurrencies. Journal of Risk and Financial Management. 2017;**10**:12. DOI: 10.3390/jrfm10020012

[7] Markowitz H. Portfolio selection. The Journal of Finance. 1952;**7**(1):77-91

[8] Elton EJ, Gruber MJ. Modern Portfolio Theory and Investment Analysis. 4ª ed. Nueva York: John Wiley & Sons; 1991

[9] Bodie Z, Kane A, Marcus AJ. Principios de Inversiones. 5ª ed. Madrid: McGraw-Hill; 2004

[10] Francis JC, Kim D. Modern Portfolio Theory: Foundations, Analysis, and New Developments. Nueva York: John Wiley and Sons; 2013

[11] Gangwal S. Analyzing the effects of adding Bitcoin to portfolio. International Journal of Economics and Management Engineering. 2016;**10**(10):3519-3532

[12] Gasser S, Eisl S, Weinmayer K. Does Bitcoin Improve Portfolio Diversification? Working Paper. Vienna: WU Vienna University of Economics and Business; 2015

[13] Kajtazi A, Moro A. The role of Bitcoin in well diversified portfolios: A comparative global study. International Review of Financial Analysis. 2019;**61**:143-157

[14] Demiguel V, Garlappi I, Uppal R. Optimal versus Naive diversification. How inefficient is the 1/N strategy? Review of Financial Studies. 2007;**22**(5):1915-1953

[15] Sharpe W. A simplified model for portfolio analysis. Management Science. 1963;**9**:277-293

[16] Bakry W, Rashid A, Al-Mohamad S, El-Kanj N. Bitcoin and portfolio diversification: A portfolio optimization approach. Journal of Risk and Financial Management. 2021;**14**(282):1-24

[17] Ho Kim J. Analyzing diversification benefits of cryptocurrencies through backfill simulation. Finance Research Letters. 2022;**50**. DOI: 10.1016/j.frl.2022.103238

[18] Liu W. Portfolio diversification across cryptocurrencies. Finance Research Letters. 2019;**29**:200-205

[19] Letho L, Chelwa G, Alhassan AL. Cryptocurrencies and portfolio diversification in an emerging market. China Finance Review International. 2022:20-50

[20] Chea E-T, Fry J. Speculative bubbles in Bitcoin markets? An empirical investigation into the fundamental value of Bitcoin. Economic Letters. 2015;**130**: 32-36

[21] Dowd K. New Private Monies. A Bit-Part Player? Howart Papers 174. Londres: Institute of Economic Affairs; 2014

[22] Parker L. The Bitcoin Bubble; Pinpointing Where Bitcoin is Among the Four Phases. New Zeland: Brave New Coin; 2017. Available from: https://bravenewcoin.com/news/the-bitcoin-bubble-pinpointing-where-bitcoin-is-among-the-four-phases/

[23] Rodrigue J-P, Comtois C, Slack B. The Geography of Transport Systems. 2nd ed. London: Routledge; 2008. ISBN 978-0-415-48324-7

[24] Podhorsky. Bursting the Bitcoin Bubble: Assessing the Fundamental Value and Social Costs of Bitcoin. ADBI Working Papers Series, n° 934. Marzo: ADB Institute; 2019

[25] Hayes A. Bitcoin price and its marginal cost of production: support for a fundamental value. Applied Economic Letters. 2019;**26**(7):554-560

[26] Mahmudov M, Puell D. Bitcoin Market-Value-to-Realized-Value (MVRV) Ratio. US: Se puede obtener; 2018. Available from: https://medium.com/adaptivecapital/bitcoin-market-value-torealized-value-mvrv-ratio-3ebc914dbaee

[27] Elmandjra Y. A Framework for Valuing Bitcoin. ARK Investment Management LLC; 2021. Available from: https://ark-invest.com/articles/analyst-research/valuing-bitcoin/

[28] Elmandjra Y, Puell D. On-Chain Data: A Framework to Evaluate Bitcoin. Diciembre, 123021 Whitepaper. St. Petersburg, FL: ARK INVEST; 2021

[29] Brunnermeier MK. Asset Pricing Under Asymmetric Information: Bubbles, Crashes, Technical Analysis and Herding. Oxford: Oxford University Press; 2001

[30] Thoma M. Bad advice, herding and bubles. Journal of Economic Methodology. 2013;**20**(1):45-55. DOI: 10.1080/1350178X.2013.774850

[31] Bouri E, Gupta G, Roubaud D. Herding behaviour in cryptocurrencies. Finance Research Letters. 2019;**29** (Junio):216-221

[32] Chang EC, Cheng JW, Khorana A. An examination of herd behaviour in equity markets: an international perspective. Journal of Banking and Finance. 2000;**24**(10):1651-1699

[33] Poyser Calderon O. Herding Behaviour in Cryptocurrency Markets. Working Paper, Noviembre. Universidad Autónoma de Barcelona, Departamento de Economía Aplicada; 2018. Available from: https://arxiv.org/pdf/1806.11348v2.pdf

[34] Jalan A, Matkovskyy R, Poti V. Shall the winning last? A study of recent bubbles and persistence. Finance Research Letters. 2022;**45**:102162

[35] Özduraka C, Karataş C. Covid-19 and the technology bubble 2.0: Evidence from DCC-MGARCH and wavelet approaches. Journal of Applied Finance & Banking. 2021;**11**(2):109-127

[36] Vidal T. FAANG Stocks Provide a Better Risk-adjusted Performance than Bitcoin. New York, USA: Cointelegraph; 2020. Available from: https://cointelegraph.com/news/faang-stocks-provide-a-better-risk-adjusted-performance-than-bitcoin

[37] Nguyen KQ. The correlation between the stock market and Bitcoin during COVID-19 and other uncertainty periods. Finance Research Letters. 2022; **46**(Parte A):102284

[38] Kim ST. Is it worth to hold bitcoin? Finance Research Letters. 2022;**44**: 102090

Chapter 7

Estimating Extreme Value at Risk Using Bayesian Markov Regime Switching GARCH-EVT Family Models

Thabani Ndlovu and Delson Chikobvu

Abstract

In this study, the performance of the Bayesian Markov regime-switching GARCH-EVT in the estimation of extreme value at risk in the BitCoin/dollar (BTC/USD) and the South African Rand/dollar (ZAR/USD) exchange rates is investigated. The goal is to capture regime switches and extreme returns to exchange rates, all to explain and compare the riskiness of BitCoin and the Rand. The Markov chain Monte Carlo method is used to estimate parameters for the GARCH family models. Using the deviance information criterion, the two regime-switching GARCH models perform better than the single-regime GARCH model when modelling volatility of the two currencies' returns. Based on the estimated value at risk figures, BitCoin is riskier than the Rand. At both 95% and 99% levels of significance, the results suggest that the MS(2)-gjrGARCH(1,1)-GEVD7 and MS(2)-sGARCH(1,1)-GPD7 are the best fitting models for both BTC/USD and ZAR/USD respectively, at both significance levels. The backtest confirms model adequacy. This information is useful to local and foreign currency traders and investors who need to fully appreciate the risk exposure when they convert their savings or investments to BitCoin instead of the South African currency, the Rand.

Keywords: Bayesian, extreme VaR, regime-switching GARCH, Markov chain Monte Carlo, extreme value theory

1. Introduction

Emerging economies' currencies, like the South African Rand, are considered risky. Currency risk is defined as the loss in value of one currency relative to another currency (most commonly against the United States dollar). The abandonment of the Bretton Wood currency system meant that the currency exchange rate is now determined by market forces, making it a volatile (risky) asset [1]. Investors' loss aversion sentiments imply a greater reaction toward losses than gains [2]. This leads to investors seeking alternative investments (diversification) to mitigate against potential losses [3]. BitCoin can be that alternative investment (diversifier) [4].

BitCoin is also a risky investment due to a lack of regulation and backing by a central bank [5]. It is still an attractive investment as witnessed by the growth its share price and volume. Recent studies have shown that BitCoin can be considered an alternative safe haven asset under certain circumstances [6–8].

The recent global financial crisis (GFC) of 2008 inspired both researchers and risk practitioners to search for better and more robust volatility models to more correctly capture financial risk. The models used prior to the GFC of 2008, collapsed in the face of stresses in the financial market. This has led to the re-visitation of the models that previously were viewed as brittle or too complicated by practitioners, all in an effort to improve the ability of the models to capture important volatility stylized facts [9–11].

The Auto-Regressive Conditional Heteroscedasticity (ARCH) and the Generalised Auto-Regressive Conditional Heteroscedasticity (GARCH) models are capable of capturing several major properties of a financial time series which are: clustering and nonlinearity, but the models fall short when the data set contains regime switches (structural changes) and fat tails. Bauwens et al. [12] showed that volatility predictions by GARCH-type models may fail to capture the true variation in volatility in the case of structural changes and regime switches in the volatility dynamics. To address this failure involves allowing the parameters of the GARCH model to vary over time according to a latent discrete Markov process commonly known as Markov switching GARCH (MS GARCH) models.

Extreme value theory (EVT) is a branch in statistical modelling that correctly captures the fat tails. EVT models quantify extreme (large fluctuations) risk. This branch of statistics was pioneered by Fisher and Tippett [13] and Pickands [14]. EVT deviates from the normality assumption that was commonly used pre global financial crisis of 2008 [15]. McNeil and Frey proposed a two stage approach to quantifying extreme VaR of financial assets. The first stage involved the fitting of GARCH family models while the second stage involved fitting EVT models to the standardised residuals extracted from the first stage.

In this study we seeks to employ the Markov regime-switching model to investigate the presence of regimes in the volatility dynamics of the returns of BitCoin (BTC) and the South African Rand (ZAR), both exchange rates are measured against the United States Dollar (USD). Furthermore, residuals from the Markov regime-switching models are extracted to fit extreme value theory (EVT) models and to estimate the extreme value at risk according to the McNeil and Frey [16] two stage method. The deviance information criterion (DIC) shall be used to select the best MS-GARCH model. Backtesting techniques shall be used to confirm model adequacy.

2. Literature review

The Markov switching GARCH models have been widely used in modelling financial data. Schwert [17] proposed a model that allowed returns switches between a high and low variance states, determined by a two state Markov process. A discrete latent variable (following a Markov process) governs the switch in the returns process. The resultant model adapts faster to variation in the dynamics of the volatility process.) Danielsson [11] noted that the stochastic process governing the volatility in crisis times is different from the one that governs in non-crisis periods hence a regime switching model could improve risk forecasts.

Hamilton and Susmel [18] and Cai [19] posited an ARCH model with Markov-switching parameters in effort to capture structural changes of the conditional variance. Gray [20] presented a tractable Markov-switching GARCH model and the extensions of this model can be found in Dueker [21], Klaassen [22], Marcucci [23], Bollen et al. [24], and Haas et al. [25].

Ardia et al. [26], Oseifuah et al. [27], and Xiaofei Wu et al. [28] empirically showed the supremacy of the Markov-switching GARCH against non-switching GARCH models in estimating risk measures like Value-at-Risk (VaR), Expected Shortfall (ES), & left-tail distribution forecasts using financial indices. Since risk measures are better estimated by a statistical distribution that best describes the returns [11] their findings suggested that the presence of regimes in the volatility dynamics of the financial returns is prevalent.

Marius et al. [29] proposed a model for forecasting VaR using a Bayesian Markov-switching GJR-GARCH [30] model with skewed Student's-*t* innovation, copula functions, and extreme value theory. Their empirical findings revealed that their proposed hybrid model (MS-GARCH EVT) captures VaR reasonably well in periods (regime) of calm and periods of crisis. According to Li [31] EVT models generally perform better than historical simulation and GARCH family models in the quantifying risk. However EVT requires that the data be identically and independently distributed (i.i.d) a feat that is commonly violated buy the financial time series [11]. To address this McNeil and Frey proposed a two stage modelling with GARCH correcting non i.i.d property and EVT capturing fat tails.

3. Methodology

3.1 The regime-switching

Let $\{r_t\}$ be a vector of demeaned log returns of assets understudy such that: $\mathbb{E}[r_t] = 0$ and $\mathbb{E}[r_t r_{t-l}] = 0$ for $l \neq 0$ and $t > 0$. According to Ardia et al. [30] the regime-switching in the conditional variance process can be expressed as:

$$r_t|(s_t = k, I_{t-1}) \sim D\left(0, \sigma_{k,t}^2, \gamma_k\right), \tag{1}$$

where I_{t-1} denotes the information set observed up to time $t-1$, $D\left(0, \sigma_{k,t}^2, \gamma_k\right)$ is the distribution of r_t with mean zero, and time-varying variance $\sigma_{k,t}^2$ and shape parameters γ_k. s_t is the integer-valued stochastic variable, defined on the space $\{1, 2, \ldots, K\}$, and characterises the regimes. The regimes (R_i) are non-overlapping such that $\left(R_i \bigcap R_j = \varnothing\right)$for any $i \neq j$.

The standardised residuals are defined as:

$$\varepsilon_{k,t} = r_t/\sigma_{k,t} \sim D(0, 1, \gamma_k), \tag{2}$$

and are i.i.d.

The integer-valued stochastic variable, s_t is assumed to evolve according to a first-order Markov chain. A two regime transition probability matrix, P, is as follows

$$P = \begin{bmatrix} p_{11} & p_{12} \\ p_{21} & p_{22} \end{bmatrix}$$

where $p_{i,j} = P[s_t = j|s_{t-1} = i]$ is the probability of a transition from regime $s_{t-1} = i$ to $s_t = j$. For $0 < p_{i,j} < 1$ under the Markov property and $\sum_{j=1}^{K} p_{i,j} = 1, \forall_{i,j} \in \{1, 2, \dots .K\}$.

According to Haas et al. [25], $\sigma^2_{k,t}$ is a GARCH-type process with K separate regimes that evolve in parallel, given by:

$$\sigma^2_{k,t} = f(r_{t-1}, \sigma^2_{k,t-1}, \theta_k), \tag{3}$$

where $f(.)$ is a function of the past returns r_{t-1}, past variance $\sigma^2_{k,t-1}$ and θ_k is the regime-dependent vector.

3.1.1 Parameter estimation

Let $\Theta = (\Phi_1, \theta_1, \dots ..\Phi_k, \theta_k, P)$ represent the vector of the model parameters. The likelihood function is:

$$L(\Theta|\mathcal{G}_T) = \prod_{t=1}^{T} f(r_t|\Theta, \mathcal{G}_{t-1}), \tag{4}$$

where $f(r_t|\Theta, \mathcal{G}_{t-1})$ is the density of r_t given past observations $\mathcal{G}_{t-1}$, and the model parameters vector Θ. For the regime switching GARCH, the conditional density of r_t is:

$$f(r_t|\Theta, \mathcal{G}_{t-1}) = \sum_{i=1}^{K} \sum_{j=1}^{K} p_{i,j} v_{i,t-1} f_D(r_t|s_t = j, \Theta, \mathcal{G}_{t-1}), \tag{5}$$

where $v_{i,t-1} = P(s_{t-1} = j, \Theta, \mathcal{G}_{t-1})$ is the Hamilton filtered probability of state i at the rime $t-1$ [18, 32].

This study seeks to apply the Bayesian statistics estimation; that is the likelihood function is combined with a prior distribution $f(\Theta)$ to get the posterior distribution $f(\Theta|\mathcal{G}_T)$ of Θ. The posterior form of the distribution is the new belief distribution on the parameters after observing the data. Ardia et al. [33] proposed:

$$f(\Theta) = f(\Phi_1, \theta_1), \dots .f(\Phi_k, \theta_k) f(P)$$

$$f(\Phi_k, \theta_k) \propto f(\Phi_k) f(\theta_k) \mathbb{I}\{(\Phi_k, \theta_k) \in CSC_k\} \ (k = 1, \dots .K)$$

$$f(\Phi_k) \propto f_N\left(\Phi_k; \mu_{\Phi_k}, diag\left(\sigma^2_{\Phi_k}\right)\right) \mathbb{I}\{(\Phi_k \in PC_k\} (k = 1, \dots .K)$$

$$f(\theta_k) \propto f_N\left(\theta_k; \mu_{\theta_k}, diag\left(\sigma^2_{\theta_k}\right)\right) \mathbb{I}\{(\theta_{k,1} > 0, \theta_{k,2} > 2\} (k = 1, \dots .K)$$

$$f(P) \propto \prod_{i=1}^{K} \left(\prod_{j=1}^{K} p_{i,j} \right) \mathbb{I}\left\{0 < p_{i,i} < 1\right\}, \tag{6}$$

where CSC_k denotes the covariance-stationarity condition and PC_k the positivity condition in regime $R_i,.\theta_{k,1}$ is the asymmetry parameter and $\theta_{k,2}$ the tail parameter of the skewed student's $t-$ distribution in regime $R_i, f_N(\bullet; \mu, \Sigma)$ denotes the multivariate normal density with mean vector μ and covariance matrix Σ. finally, $\mu_\bullet$ and $\sigma^2_\bullet$ are vectors of prior means and variances .

3.1.2 The regime switching GARCH model is given by

$$\sigma_{k,t}^2 = \alpha_{0,k} + \alpha_{1,k} r_{t-1}^2 + \beta_k \sigma_{k,t-1}^2, \tag{7}$$

where $k = 1, \dots, K$ regimes, $\Theta_k - (\alpha_{0,k}, \alpha_{1,k}, \beta_k)^T$. Parameter restrictions are $\alpha_{0,k} > 0, \alpha_{1,k} > 0$, and $\beta_k \geq 0$. To ensure stationarity in each regime, we require $\alpha_{1,k} + \beta_k < 1$.

3.1.3 The regime switching exponential GARCH (EGARCH) model is given by

$$\ln\left(\sigma_{k,t}^2\right) = \alpha_{0,k} + \alpha_{1,k}\left(\left|\eta_{k,t-1}\right| - \mathbb{E}\left[\left|\eta_{k,t-1}\right|\right]\right) + \alpha_{2,k}\eta_{k,t-1} + \beta_k \ln\left(\sigma_{k,t-1}^2\right), \tag{8}$$

for $k = 1, \dots, K$, where the expectation $\mathbb{E}\left[\left|\eta_{k,t-1}\right|\right]$ is taken with the respect to the conditional distribution of the regime k. The parameters to be estimated are $\Theta_k = (\alpha_{0,k}, \alpha_{1,k}, \alpha_{2,k}, \beta_k)^T$. Positivity is ensured by the model specification.

3.1.4 The regime switching GJR-GARCH model by Glosten et al. [34] is given by

$$\sigma_{k,t}^2 = \alpha_{0,k} + (\alpha_{1,k} + \alpha_{2,k}\mathbb{I}\{r_t < 0\}) r_{t-1}^2 + \beta_k \sigma_{k,t-1}^2, \tag{9}$$

for $k = 1, \dots, K$, where $\mathbb{I}\{.\}$ is an indicator function taking the value one, if the residual is smaller than zero and the value zero if the residual is not smaller than zero. The parameters to be estimated are $\Theta_k = (\alpha_{0,k}, \alpha_{1,k}, \alpha_{2,k}, \beta_k)^T$. For variance to be positive, we require that $\alpha_{0,k} > 0, \alpha_{1,k} > 0, \alpha_{2,k} \geq 0$ and $\beta_k \geq 0$. To ensure stationarity of each regime, we require that $(\alpha_{1,k} + \alpha_{2,k}\mathbb{I}\{r_t < 0\}) r_{t-1}^2 + \beta_k \sigma_{k,t-1}^2 < 1$.

3.2 Extreme value theory

Let y_i be the standardised residuals that are extracted from the GARCH models. The peak over threshold (POT) data selection approach used to fit the Generalised Pareto Distribution (GPD), and the block maxima (BM) data selection approach for fitting the Generalised Extreme Value Distribution (GEVD) are used to model the standardised residuals from the selected GARCH models.

3.2.1 The Generalised Pareto Distribution (GPD)

Balkema and deHaan [35] and Pickands [14] showed that for a threshold u that is large enough, the exceedances can be estimated by the GPD. The Generalised Pareto Distribution is defined as follows:

$$G_{\xi,\beta}(y) = \begin{cases} 1 - \left(1 + \frac{\xi(y-u)}{\beta}\right)^{-1/\xi} & \text{if } \xi \neq 0 \\ 1 - \exp\left(-\left(\frac{y-u}{\beta}\right)\right) & \text{if } \xi = 0 \end{cases}, \tag{10}$$

where $y > u$, $y - u$ is the exceedance, and $0 \leq y \leq {-\beta}/{\xi}$, $\beta > 0, f_{\xi,\beta}(y)$ is a GPD with the shape parameter or tail index ξ, a scale parameter β and a threshold u. The value of ξ shows how heavy the tail is, with a bigger positive value value$(\xi \geq 0)$ indicating a heavy tail, $\xi < 0$ indicates a bounded tail. $\xi = 0$ indicates a light tail.

The density function is given as:

$$g_{\xi,\beta}(y) = \begin{cases} \frac{1}{\beta}\left(1 + \frac{\xi(y-u)}{\beta}\right)^{-1-\frac{1}{\xi}} \text{ if } \xi \neq 0 \\ , \\ \exp\left(-\left(\frac{y-u}{\beta}\right)\right) \text{ if } \xi = 0 \end{cases} \tag{11}$$

Parameter estimation of GPD:

Let u be a sufficiently high threshold, assuming n observations and y such that $y_i - u \geq 0$, the subsample $\{y_1 - u, \ldots, y_n - u\}$ has an underlying distribution of a GPD, where $y_i - u \geq 0$ for $\xi \geq 0$, $0 \leq y_i - u \leq -\frac{\beta}{\xi}$, then the logarithm of the probability density function of

$y_i - u$ is:

$$\ln(f(y_i - u)) = \begin{cases} -\ln(\beta) - \frac{1+\xi}{\xi}\ln\left(1 + \xi\left(\frac{y_i - u}{\beta}\right)\right) \textit{ if } \xi \neq 0 \\ , \\ -\ln(\beta) - \frac{1}{\beta}(y_i - u) \textit{ if } \xi = 0 \end{cases} \tag{12}$$

Then the log-likelihood $l(\xi, \beta | y_i - u)$ of the joint density of the n observations is:

$$l(\xi, \beta | y_i - u) = \begin{cases} -n\ln(\beta) - \frac{1+\xi}{\xi}\sum_{i=1}^{n}\ln\left(1 + \xi\left(\frac{y_i - u}{\beta}\right)\right) \textit{ if } \xi \neq 0 \\ , \\ -n\ln(\beta) - \frac{1}{\beta}\sum_{i=1}^{n}(y_i - u) \textit{ if } \xi = 0 \end{cases} \tag{13}$$

One obtains the parameters (ξ, β) by maximising the log-likelihood function of the subsample under a suitable threshold u. Numerical methods are used to arrive at the maximum likelihood estimates.

3.2.2 The Generalised Extreme Value Distribution (GEVD)

The GEVD is the limiting distribution of normalised block maxima of a sequence of independent identically distributed random variables [13] and [36]. The GEVD is given as follows:

$$G_{\xi,\mu,\sigma}(y) = \begin{cases} \exp\left\{-\left(1+\xi\left(\frac{y-\mu}{\sigma}\right)\right)\right\}, \text{if } \xi \neq 0 \\ , \\ , \\ \exp\left\{-\exp\left(-\left(\frac{y-\mu}{\sigma}\right)\right)\right\}, \text{if } \xi \to 0 \end{cases} , \tag{14}$$

with $\xi \neq 0, \sigma > 0$ and $1+\xi\left(\frac{y-\mu}{\sigma}\right) > 0$.

The probability density function, obtained as the derivative of the above distribution function, is given by:

$$g_{\xi,\mu,\sigma}(y) = \begin{cases} \frac{1}{\sigma}\left(1+\xi\left(\frac{y-\mu}{\sigma}\right)\right) \exp\left\{-^{\left(1+\xi\left(\frac{y-\mu}{\sigma}\right)\right)}\right\} \text{ if } \xi \neq 0 \\ , \\ , \\ \frac{1}{\sigma}\exp\left\{-\exp\left(-\left(\frac{y-\mu}{\sigma}\right)\right)\right\}\exp\left(-\left(\frac{y-\mu}{\sigma}\right)\right) \text{ if } \xi \to 0 \end{cases} \tag{15}$$

where μ and σ are the location and scale parameters respectively.

The shape parameter ξ is also known as the extreme value index (EVI).

Parameter estimation:

Let $Y_1, \ldots.., Y_m$ are independent block maxima variables following the GEVD, the log-likelihood for the parameters, when $\xi \neq 0$, is

$$l = \begin{cases} -m\ln(\sigma) - \left(1+\frac{1}{\xi}\right)\sum_{i=1}^{m}\ln\left[1+\xi\left(\frac{y_i-\mu}{\sigma}\right)\right] - \sum_{i=1}^{m}\left[1+\xi\left(\frac{y_i-\mu}{\sigma}\right)\right]^{-\frac{1}{\xi}} \text{if } \xi \neq 0 \\ , \\ , \\ -m\ln(\sigma) - \sum_{i=1}^{m}\exp\left[-\left(\frac{y_i-\mu}{\sigma}\right)\right] - \sum_{i=1}^{m}\left(\frac{y_i-\mu}{\sigma}\right) \text{ if } \xi \to 0 \end{cases} \tag{16}$$

Maximisation of the above function with respect to the parameters vector (ξ, μ, σ), leads to the maximum likelihood estimates for the entire GEVD family [37].

3.3 Value at risk

To quantify the value at risk, for tail probability p, and total sample size n.

For a GPD with MLEs $(\hat{\beta}, \hat{\sigma}, \hat{\xi})$, threshold u and N_u the number of exceedances, VaR is given by:

$$V\hat{a}R_p(y_t) = \begin{cases} u + \frac{\hat{\beta}}{\hat{\xi}}\left\{1 - [-n\ln(1-p)]^{-\hat{\xi}}\right\} \text{ if } \hat{\xi} \neq 0 \\ u - \hat{\sigma}\ln(-n\ln(1-p)) \text{ if } \hat{\xi} = 0 \end{cases} \tag{17}$$

for a GEVD with maximum likelihood estimates $(\hat{\mu}, \hat{\sigma}, \hat{\xi})$,

$$\hat{VaR_p}(y_t) = \begin{cases} u + \frac{\hat{\sigma}}{\hat{\xi}}\left\{\left(\frac{n}{N_u}p\right)^{-\hat{\xi}} - 1\right\} \text{ if } \hat{\xi} \neq 0 \\ u - \hat{\beta}\ln\left(\frac{n}{N_u}(1-p)\right) \text{ if } \hat{\xi} = 0 \end{cases} \tag{18}$$

Finally, according to McNeil and Frey [16], the VaR of the asset is computed using the following formula:

$$VaR_p(r_t) = \mu_t + \sigma_{kt}.VaR_p(y_t), \tag{19}$$

where is $\mu_t = 0$ by demeaning the returns σ_{kt} is estimated from the volatility model (Markov switching Generalised Auto-Regressive Conditional Heteroscedasticity (MS-GARCH)). $VaR_p(r_t)$ is the p percentile of the standardised residuals. The riskiness of the asset is expressed through $VaR_p(y_t)$, hence the modelling of the residuals. This is especially important when modelling extreme risk.

4. Results and discussions

Quantitative data was collected and modelled so as to achieve the set objectives. Currency data was obtained from the finance sector website www.investing.com/currencies. The currencies considered are; the South African Rand against the US dollar (ZAR/USD) and the BitCoin against US dollar (BTC/USD). The data was analysed in an R-programming environment using the MSGARCH, evir and rugarch packages. The daily exchange rates considered were from 01 January 2015 to 30 June 2021. The log returns were calculated and used to do the modelling.

In **Figures 1** and **2**, the trends in the mean and variance, confirm non-stationarity of the exchange rates prices. The log returns look stationary, around the zero-mean, although volatility clustering occurs, which is common with financial data. Isolated extreme returns are visible, caused by shocks in the financial markets.

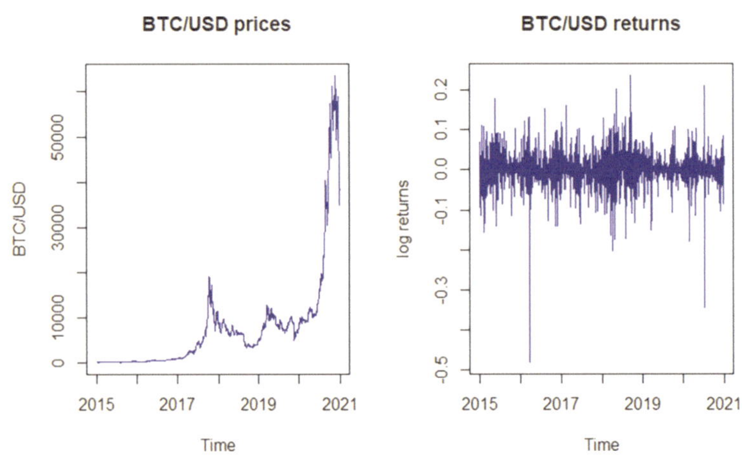

Figure 1.
Price of BTC/USD (left) and returns (right).

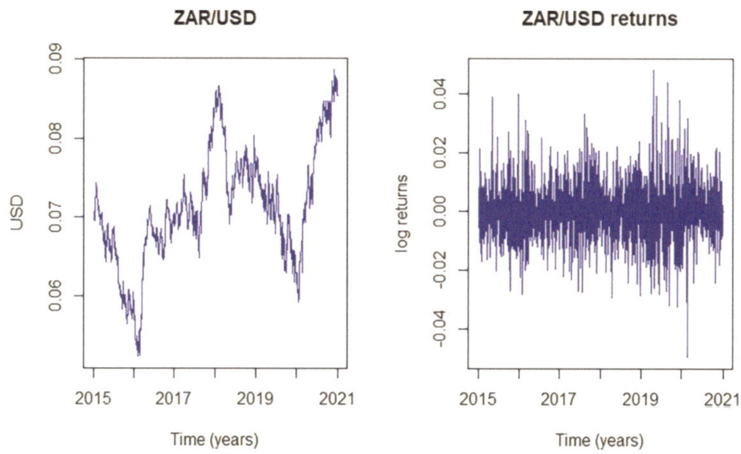

Figure 2.
Price of ZAR/USD (left) and returns (right).

Tests for Normality, autocorrelation, and heteroscedasticity are presented in **Table 1**. The Jarque-Bera test rejects normality at a 5% level of significance, implying that the use of heavy-tailed distributions could be ideal when analysing the currency returns.

The Ljung-Box test statistic for the for the BitCoin returns, rejects the null hypothesis that returns are i.i.d, hence the two-step approach is recommended to help deal with the autocorrelation.

The ARCH LM test rejects the claim of no ARCH effects at the 5% level of significance, suggesting the use of GARCH family models should be considered when

	Observations	Mean	Median	Maximum	Minimum	Skewness	Kurtosis
BitCoin	2370	0.001990	0.001757	0.237220	−0.480904	−0.994382	16.15451
Rand	1694	−0.000125	0.000000	0.049546	−0.048252	−0.264130	4.121644

Test for normality, autocorrelation and heteroscedasticity				
Test	**BitCoin**		**Rand**	
	Statistic	**p-value**	**Statistic**	**p-value**
Jarque-Bera	17478.40	0.000000	108.4967	0.000000
Ljung-Box	11.7	0.0006249	0.40504	0.5245
ARCH LM test	52.87	4.345e−07	70.789	2.28e-10
Test for unit root and stationarity				
Unit root test	**BitCoin**		**Rand**	
	Statistic	**p-value**	**Statistic**	**p-value**
ADF test	−52.20130	0.0001	−40.47263	0.0000
PP test	−52.10963	0.0001	−40.47011	0.0000
KPSS test	0.092067	0.347000	0.090747	0.347000

Table 1.
Descriptive statistics of exchange rate price returns. Reproduced with permission from Ndlovu and Chikobvu [38].

analysing the above-mentioned return series. The KPSS test results confirm the stationarity of both returns since all p-values are greater than 0.05.

4.1 Markov switching GARCH models

Both the single regime and two regimes switching versions of GARCH, eGARCH, and gjr-GARCH were fitted using the MSGARCH package created by Ardia et al. [33]. The choice of two regimes is influenced by the work of [39]. Both Normal and Student's t residuals for this set of models resulted in a total of 12 models for each currency as presented in **Table 2**.

4.1.1 Deviance Information Criterion (DIC)

The best fit model was selected using the Deviance Information Criteria statistic, proposed by Spiegelhalter et al. [40].

For both series the two–regime switching models gave the lowest DIC, confirming the presence of structural breaks in the data. For the BitCoin returns the MS(2)-gjrGARCH with Student's t residuals is the best fit while for Rand, the MS(2)-sGARCH with student' t residuals gave the least Deviance Information Criteria.

4.1.2 Two-regime gjrGARCH with Student's t *residuals for BTC/USD*

The results for the two-regime gjrGARCH model for the BitCoin are presented in **Table 3**.

Column 5 shows the Relative Numerical Efficiencies (RNE) of the estimates. Lower values of RNE are desirable as they show that our samples are independent [41]. All values are low and therefore one can rely on the estimates for inference.

Parameter estimates indicate that the evolution of the volatility process is heterogeneous across the two regimes. The two regimes report different unconditional volatility levels which are 0.9208993 and 0.5949609 for the first and second regime

Model	BitCoin	Rand
Single regime GARCH-norm	−9025.5756	−10770.6033
Single regime GARCH-std	−9420.0605	−10790.0914
Single regime eGARCH-norm	−9108.5423	−10787.4882
Single regime eGARCH-std	−9492.1716	−10794.7034
Single regime gjrGARCH-nor	−9021.653	−10766.0122
Single regime gjrGARCH-std	−9417.8438	−10781.5634
MS(2)-GARCH-norm	−9355.4633	−10792.099
MS(2)-GARCH-std	−9473.3317	−10799.1979
MS(2)-eGARCH-norm	−9351.0697	−10788.0544
MS(2)-eGARCH-std	−9395.7586	−10787.3264
MS(2)-gjrGARCH-norm	−9365.0784	−10773.2
MS(2)-gjrGARCH-std	−9505.5685	−10790.0478

Table 2.
The DIC statistic for each model under consideration.

Parameter	Mean	SD	SE	TSSE	RNE
alpha0_1	0.0018	0.0010	0.0000	0.0001	0.0502
alpha1_1	0.1456	0.0926	0.0029	0.0095	0.0944
alpha2_1	0.0023	0.0028	0.0001	0.0003	0.1162
beta_1	0.2258	0.4083	0.0129	0.0583	0.0490
nu_1	6.4674	4.8511	0.1534	0.8763	0.0306
alpha0_2	0.0005	0.0010	0.0000	0.0001	0.0516
alpha1_2	0.0393	0.0736	0.0023	0.0093	0.0621
alpha2_2	0.0081	0.0056	0.0002	0.0013	0.0186
beta_2	0.7762	0.4063	0.0128	0.0579	0.0492
nu_2	3.0882	1.7606	0.0557	0.2435	0.0523
P_1_1	0.9825	0.0060	0.0002	0.0004	0.2602
P_2_1	0.0185	0.0052	0.0002	0.0004	0.2034
$P(S_{t+1} = 1 \mid S_t = 1)$			0.9825		
$P(S_{t+1} = 2 \mid S_t = 1)$			0.0175		
$P(S_{t+1} = 1 \mid S_t = 2)$			0.0185		
$P(S_{t+1} = 2 \mid S_t = 2)$			0.9815		

Table 3.
The MCMC parameter estimates of the MS(2)-gjrGARCH with STD residuals for the BitCoin.

respectively. The volatility persistence in first regime is $\alpha_{1,1} + 0.5\alpha_{2,1} + \beta_1 \approx 0.37$ while the second regime gives $\alpha_{1,2} + 0.5\alpha_{2,2} + \beta_2 \approx 0.82$. Also the results show stable probabilities of 0.5135 and 0.4865 for the low and high regime, respectively. This implies the low regime is with a small margin dominant compared to the high volatility regime.

The smoothed probability of the high volatility regimes together with the filtered conditional volatility for the two-regime gjrGARCH for the BitCoin is shown in **Figure 3**.

4.1.3 Two-regime GARCH with Student's t *residuals for Rand*

The result for the two-regime sGARCH-std model for the Rand is presented in **Table 4**. Column 5 shows the Relative Numerical Efficiencies (RNE) of the estimates.

Lower values of RNE are desirable as they show that our samples are independent [41]. All values are moderately low and therefore we can rely on the estimates for inference.

Parameter estimates indicate that the evolution of the volatility process is heterogeneous across the two regimes. The two regimes report different unconditional volatility levels which are 0.1355 and 0.2010 for the first and second regimes respectively. The volatility persistence in the first regime is $\alpha_{1,1} + \beta_1 \approx 0.82$ while the second regime gives $\alpha_{1,2} + \beta_2 \approx 0.39$. Also, the results show stable probabilities of 0.6452 and 0.3548 for the low and high regimes, respectively. This implies the low regime is dominant compared to the high volatility regime.

The smoothed probability of the high volatility regimes together with the filtered conditional volatility for the two-regime sGARCH for the ZAR/USD returns is shown in **Figure 4**.

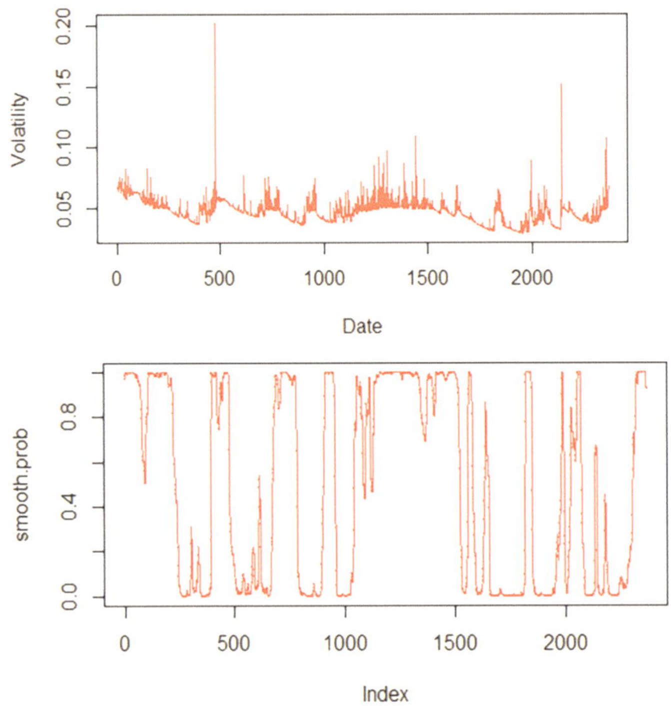

Figure 3.
The conditional volatility and the Smoothed probabilities of the high volatility regime for the BitCoin.

Parameter	Mean	SD	SE	TSSE	RNE
alpha0_1	0.0000	0.0000	0.0000	0.0000	0.1677
alpha1_1	0.0722	0.0351	0.0011	0.0022	0.2591
beta_1	0.7506	0.0583	0.0018	0.0044	0.1743
nu_1	60.7986	18.9997	0.6008	0.9908	0.3678
alpha0_2	0.0001	0.0000	0.0000	0.0000	0.1517
alpha1_2	0.1105	0.0559	0.0018	0.0030	0.3491
beta_2	0.2818	0.1572	0.0050	0.0127	0.1521
nu_2	16.8238	7.0276	0.2222	0.5612	0.1568
P_1_1	0.9883	0.0051	0.0002	0.0003	0.3485
P_2_1	0.0212	0.0112	0.0004	0.0006	0.2991
$P(S_{t+1} = 1 \| S_t = 1)$			0.9883		
$P(S_{t+1} = 2 \| S_t = 1)$			0.0117		
$P(S_{t+1} = 1 \| S_t = 2)$			0.0212		
$P(S_{t+1} = 2 \| S_t = 2)$			0.9788		

Table 4.
The MCMC parameter estimates of the MS(2)-sGARCH with STD residuals for the Rand.

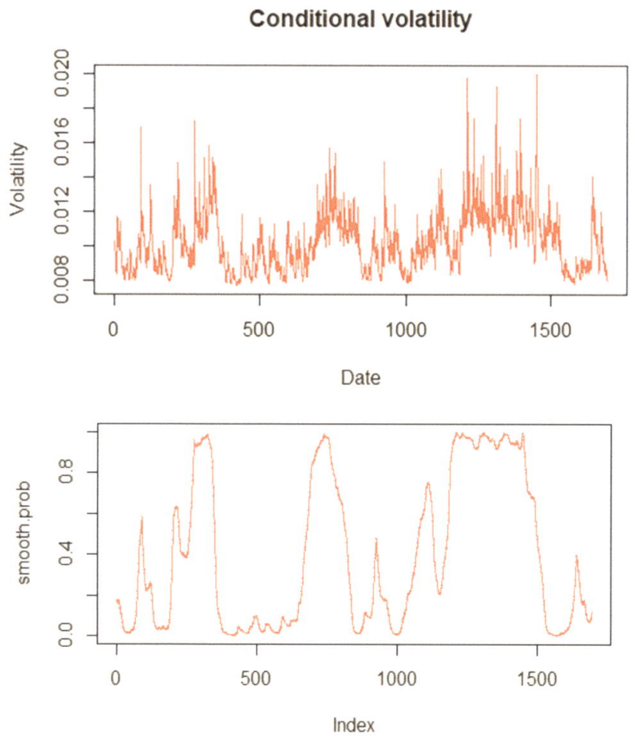

Figure 4.
The conditional volatility and the smoothed probabilities of the high volatility regime for the Rand.

4.2 GARCH-EVT models

The best fit models selected using DIC statistic were used to extract standardise residuals, which were in turn used to fit the Generalised Pareto Distribution (GPD) models and Generalised Extreme Value Distributions (GEVD), for computation of extreme value at risk and comparisons thereafter.

4.2.1 Model fitting for BitCoin

To fit the Generalised Pareto Distribution, the choice of a threshold u is critical. This threshold, determines the number of extremes, N_u that would be used for modelling GPD. "As a rule of thumb also suggests that it is ideal to choose the threshold that gives about 100 observations for fitting of the Pareto distribution when the data set is large enough" McNeil and Frey [16].

According to the mean excess plots in **Figure 5**, a threshold of between 0.3 and 1.2 seems to be a reasonable choice. In this study we used the 70th, 80th, and 90th percentile to extract the extremes. They all provided reasonable choices as they yielded enough data points for the analyses (as presented in **Table 5**).

To fit the GEVD, block maxima are selected. The maximum observation in each block is then used for further analysis. The parameters of the GEVD were estimated using weekly, fortnightly, and triweekly block sizes of 7, 14, and 21 days respectively for BitCoin are presented in **Table 6**.

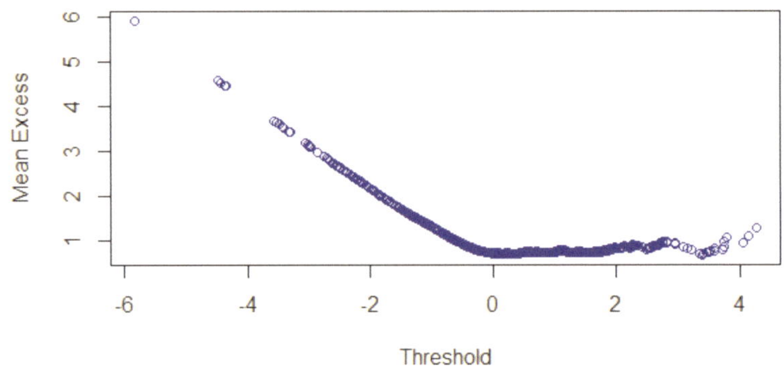

Figure 5.
Mean excess function for BitCoin returns.

Model	Threshold	Number of exceedances	$\hat{\xi}$	$Se(\hat{\xi})$	$\hat{\beta}$	$Se(\hat{\beta})$
GPD70	0.3153252	711	0.03249619	0.03912178	0.54737246	0.02965833
GPD80	0.5381404	474	0.02650686	0.04717943	0.55975277	0.03685255
GPD90	0.9272855	237	0.03193045	0.06902576	0.56771192	0.05379748

Table 5.
GPD estimates for BitCoin.

Model	Number of maxima	$\hat{\xi}$	$Se(\hat{\xi})$	$\hat{\sigma}$	$Se(\hat{\sigma})$	$\hat{\mu}$	$Se(\hat{\mu})$
GEV7	339	0.118126	0.0478093	0.501676	0.0242079	0.713575	0.0314231
GEV14	170	0.108604	0.0648413	0.534065	0.0358519	1.047110	0.0469099
GEV21	113	0.053869	0.0733003	0.592139	0.0468834	1.249844	0.0631369

Table 6.
Estimates for BitCoin.

4.2.2 Model fitting for Rand

By observing **Figure 6**, a threshold of between 0.5 and 1.8 seems to be a reasonable choice for negative returns. In this study, we used the 70th, 80th' and 90th percentile

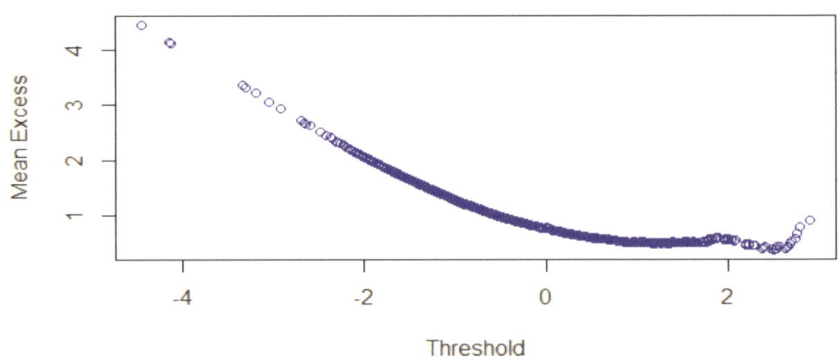

Figure 6.
Mean excess function for Rand returns.

were selected. They all provided reasonable choices as they yielded enough data points for analyses and all fell within the above range.

The MLE parameter estimates of the GPD are presented in the **Table 7**.

To fit the GEVD, block maxima are selected. The maximum observation in each block is then used for further analysis. The parameters of the GEVD were estimated using weekly (Monday to Friday), fortnightly, and triweekly block sizes of 7, 14, and 21 days respectively for the Rand are presented in **Table 8**. The readings for Saturday and Sunday were taken as zero, and they do not affect the maxima for the block.

Table 9 shows value at risk statistics are computed at 95% and 99% confidence levels for both exchange rates understudy. Higher VaR values for BitCoin suggest that it is riskier than Rand since it has a higher value at risk per USD invested in each currency. At 99% significance levels, BitCoin has an average of 2.38% and 4.11% for MS-gjrGARCH(1,1)-GPD and MS-gjrGARCH(1,1)-GEVD, respectively; this is slightly higher than the averages of 2.28% and 3.42% for the Rand, respectively. In monetary terms, at 99% level significance, an investor holding on to BitCoin is likely to lose extremes of approximately 4.11BTC/USD per 100BTC/USD invested compared to the 3.42Rand/USD likely to be lost by one holding on to the Rand, confirming the high risk associated with BitCoin.

Model	Threshold	Number of exceedances	$\hat{\xi}$	$Se(\hat{\xi})$	$\hat{\sigma}$	$Se(\hat{\sigma})$
GPD70	0.5127883	508	−0.097589	0.03024782	0.65871725	0.03525891
GPD80	0.8253023	339	−0.020726	0.04962634	0.52896076	0.03890997
GPD90	1.181104	170	−0.013318	0.06980646	0.51928781	0.05385240

Table 7.
GPD estimates for ZAR/USD.

Model	Number of maxima	$\hat{\xi}$	$Se(\hat{\xi})$	$\hat{\sigma}$	$Se(\hat{\sigma})$	$\hat{\mu}$	$Se(\hat{\mu})$
GEV7	339	−0.0579	0.030827	0.559786	0.023468	0.841658	0.033415
GEV14	170	−0.0562	0.042645	0.557080	0.032759	1.199244	0.046847
GEV21	113	−0.0180	0.059649	0.518711	0.038625	1.410612	0.054108

Table 8.
GEVD estimates for ZAR/USD.

Model	BTC/USD		Model	ZAR/USD	
	95%	99%		95%	99%
MS-GPD70	1.595405	2.419146	MS-GPD70	1.3252	2.283829
MS-GPD80	1.548466	2.362027	MS-GPD80	1.328556	2.283386
MS-GPD90	1.54121	2.360441	MS-GPD90	1.32518	2.283745
MS-GEV7	2.49851	3.779234	MS-GEV7	2.3692	3.102301
MS-GEV14	2.919118	4.233949	MS-GEV14	2.723047	3.457184
MS-GEV21	3.157133	4.340975	MS-GEV21	2.910692	3.700328

Table 9.
VaR estimates.

4.3 Back testing results for value at risk

The VaR estimates from the fitted MS(2)-gjrGARCH(1,1)-GPD, MS(2)-gjrGARCH (1,1)-GEV for the BitCoin and MS(2)-sGARCH(1,1)-GPD, MS(2)-GARCH(1,1)-GEV type family models are back tested using the Kupiec [42] likelihood test. The results are compared with the non-hybrid GPD and GEV. The p-values of each test are presented in **Table 10**.

Based on the p-values presented in **Table 10**, the adequacy of the fitted models is largely confirmed since the observed p-statistics are greater than 0.05. The model with the highest p-value is considered to be superior, and hence it is adopted for use by financial risk analysts in estimating currency VaR and ascertaining their trading and investment strategies.

The Kupiec test suggests that the MS(2)-gjrGARCH(1,1)-GEVD7 and MS(2)-sGARCH(1,1)-GPD7 are the best fitted models for both BitCoin and Rand investments respectively, at both significance levels.

5. Conclusion and recommendations

In this study, the estimation and performance of selected Bayesian Markov regime-switching GARCH methodologies were explored using the BitCoin and Rand data. Three univariate MSGARCH-based models were explored and implemented, with the Normal and the Student's t error distributions, and their deviance information criterion statistic was used to select the best fitting model. The standardised residuals of the selected best fit model were extracted and used to fit Generalised Pareto Distributions and Generalised Extreme Value Distributions before being used in the estimation of the VaR.

Furthermore, the estimated VaR is validated using the backtest procedure. The backtest results show that the hybrid two regimes MSGARCH-GPD performs better than single regimes models. At both 95% and 99% levels of significance, the Kupiec test suggests that the MS(2)-gjrGARCH(1,1)-GEVD7 and MS(2)-sGARCH(1,1)-GPD7 are the best fitted models for both BitCoin and Rand respectively, at both significance levels.

Based on VaR statistics, it is clear that the BitCoin is riskier than the South African Rand. These results are helpful to forex risk managers and investors in helping understand the switches in the risks during crises and non-crisis times. Particularly

Model	BitCoin		Model	Rand	
	95%	99%		95%	99%
MS-GPD70	0.6733027	0.3148938	MS-GPD70	0.3239718	0.6217179
MS-GPD80	0.7426442	0.3148938	MS-GPD80	0.7984784	0.6217179
MS-GPD90	0.6733027	0.3148938	MS-GPD90	0.7146211	0.6217179
MS-GEV7	0.8111915	0.7461146	MS-GEV7	0.6159644	0.8281038
MS-GEV14	0.5865878	0.5588778	MS-GEV14	0.8615834	0.5588778
MS-GEV21	0.5736501	0.9002366	MS-GEV21	0.2106977	0.9002366

Table 10.
p-*values of the Kupiec's likelihood test.*

when the market enters a turbulent time, they may consider staying clear of the risky investments for which they have no appetite. Switches in volatility improve robust pricing of financial assets, and equities and make adequate risk-based capital requirements more rational.

Abbreviations

ARCH	Auto-Regressive Conditional Heteroscedasticity
BCBS	Basel Committee on Banking Supervision
BTC	Bit Coin
DIC	deviance information criterion
ES	expected shortfall
EVT	extreme value theory
GARCH	Generalised Auto-Regressive Conditional Heteroscedasticity
GPD	Generalised Pareto Distribution
GEVD	Generalised Extreme Value Distribution
GJR	Glosten, Jagannathan, and Runkle
MCMC	Markov Chain Monte Carlo
POT	peak over threshold
VaR	value at risk
ZAR	South African Rand

Author details

Thabani Ndlovu* and Delson Chikobvu
Department of Mathematical Statistics and Actuarial Science, University of the Free State, South Africa

*Address all correspondence to: thabsndlovu89@gmail.com

References

[1] Van Der Merwe E. Exchange Rate Management Policies in South Africa: Recent Experience and Prospects. South African Reserve Bank Occasional Paper No. 8. June 1995. Pretoria, South Africa. 1996. Available from: https://books.google.com.hk/books/about/Exchange_Rate_Management_Policies_in_Sou.html?id=E7AxAQAAIAAJ&redir_esc=y [Accessed: 31 March 2023]

[2] Tversky A, Kahneman D. Loss aversion in riskless choice: A reference-dependent model. The Quarterly Journal of Economics. 1991;**106**(4):1039-1061

[3] Conlon T, Corbet S, McGee RJ. Are cryptocurrencies a safe haven for equity markets? An international perspective from the COVID-19 pandemic. Research in International Business and Finance. 2020;**54**(C):S0275531920304438. Available from: https://EconPapers.repec.org/RePEc:eee:riibaf:v:54:y:2020:i:c:s0275531920304438

[4] Huang Y, Duan K, Mishra T. Is bitcoin really more than a diversifier? A pre- and post-COVID-19 analysis. Financial Research Letters. 2021;**43**: 102016. DOI: 10.1016/j.frl.2021.102016

[5] Kaseke F, Ramroop S, Mhwambi H. A comparison of the stylised facts of bitcoin, ethereum and the JSE stock returns. African Finance Journal. 2021; **23**:50-64

[6] Cocco L, Tonelli R, Marchesi M. BitCoin as a safe haven during COVID-19 disease. Future Internet. 2022;**14**:98. DOI: 10.3390/fi14040098

[7] Jeribi A, Jena SK, Lahiani A. Are cryptocurrencies a backstop for the stock market in a covid-19-led financial crisis? Evidence from the NARDL approach. International Journal of Financial Studies. 2021;**9**(3):33. DOI: 10. 3390/ijfs9030033

[8] Yan Y, Lei Y, Wang Y. BitCoin as a safe-haven asset and a medium of exchange. Axioms. 2022;**11**:415. DOI: 10.3390/axioms11080415

[9] Makatjane K, Moroke N. Predicting extreme daily regime shifts in financial time series exchange/Johannesburg stock exchange—All share index. International Journal of Financial Studies. 2021;**9**:18. DOI: 10.3390/ijfs9020018

[10] Makhwiting MR, Sigauke C, Lesaoana M. Modelling tail behavior of returns using the generalised extreme value distribution. Economics, Management, and Financial Markets. 2014;**9**:41

[11] Danielsson J. Financial Risk Forecasting. London, UK: Wiley; 2011

[12] Bauwens L, Backer B, A, D. A Bayesian method of change-point estimation with recurrent regimes: Application to GARCH models. Journal of Empirical Finance. 2014;**29**:207-229. DOI: 10.1016/j.jempfin.2014.06.008

[13] Fisher RA, Tippett LHC. Limiting forms of the frequency distribution of the largest or smallest member of a sample. Mathematical Proceedings of the Cambridge Philosophical Society. 1928; **24**(2):180-190

[14] Pickands J. Statistical inference using extreme order statistics. Annals of Statistics. 1975;**3**:119-131

[15] MacKenzie D, Spears T. The formula that killed wall street': The gaussian copula and modelling practices in investment banking. Social Studies of Science. 2014;**44**:393-417

[16] McNeil AJ, Frey R. Estimation of tail-related risk measures for heteroscedastic

financial time series: An extreme value approach. Journal of Empirical Finance. 2000;**7**(3):271-300

[17] Schwert G. Why does stock market volatility change over time? Journal of Finance. 1989;**44**:1115-1153

[18] Hamilton JD, Susmel R. Autoregressive conditional heteroskedasticity and changes in regime. Journal of Econometrics. 1994; **64**(1–2):307-333

[19] Cai J. Markov model of unconditional variance in ARCH. Journal of Business and Economics Statistics. 1994;**12**:309-316

[20] Gray S. Modeling the conditional distribution of interest rates as a regime-switching process. Journal of Financial Economics. 1996;**42**:27-62

[21] Dueker M. Markov switching in GARCH processes in mean reverting stock market volatility. Journal of Business and Economics Statistics. 1997; **15**:26-34

[22] Klaassen F. Improving GARCH volatility forecasts with regime-switching GARCH. Empirical Economics. 2002;**27**:363-394

[23] Marcucci J. Forecasting stock market volatility with regime-switching GARCH models. Studies in Nonlinear Dynamics and Econometrics. 2005;**9**:1-53

[24] Bollen S, Gray N, Whaley R. Regime-switching in foreign exchange rates: Evidence from currency option prices. Journal of Econometrics. 2000; **94**:239-276

[25] Haas M, Mittnik S, Paolella M. A new approach to Markov-switching GARCH models. Journal of Financial Econometrics. 2004;**2**:493-530

[26] Ardia D, Bluteau K, Boudt K, Catania L. Forecasting risk with Markov-switching GARCH models: A large-scale performance study. International Journal of Forecasting. 2018;**34**(2018):733-747

[27] Oseifuah EK, Korkpoe CH. A Markov regime switching approach to estimating the volatility of Johannesburg stock exchange (JSE) returns. Investment Management and Financial Innovations. 2019;**16**(1):215-225. DOI: 10.21511/imfi.16(1).2019.17

[28] Wu X, Zhu S, Zhou J. Research on RMB exchange rate volatility risk based on MSGARCH-VaR model. Hindawi Discrete Dynamics in Nature and Society. 2020:Article ID 8719574. 10.1155/2020/8719574

[29] Marius GS, Haslifah MH, Hongsheng D. Refining value-at-risk estimates using a Bayesian Markov-switching GJR-GARCH copula-EVT model. PLoS One. 2018;**13**(6):e0198753. DOI: 10.1371/journal.pone.0198753

[30] Ardia D, Bluteau K, Boudt K, Catania L, Trottier D. Markov-switching GARCH models in R: The MSGARCH package. Journal of Statistical Software. Forthcoming. 2016. DOI: 10.2139/ssrn.2845809

[31] Li L. A Comparative Study of GARCH and EVT Model in Modeling Value-at-Risk. MPRA Paper 85645. Germany: University Library of Munich; 2017

[32] Hamilton J. A new approach to the economic analysis of nonstationary time series and the business cycle. Econometrica. 1989;**57**(2):357-384

[33] Ardia D, Bluteau K, Boudt K, Catania L, Trottier D. Markov-switching GARCH models in R: The MSGARCH package.

Journal of Statistical Software. 2019;**91** (4). DOI: 10.18637/jss.v091.i04

[34] Glosten L, Jagannathan R, Runkle D. On the relation between the expected value and the volatility of the nominal excess return on stocks. Journal of Finance. 1993;**XLVIII**:1779-1801

[35] Balkema B, deHaan L. Residual lifetime at a great age. Annals of Probability. 1974;**2**:792-804

[36] Gnedenko BV. Sur la distribution limite du terme maximum of d'unesérie Aléatorie. Annals of Mathematics. 1943;**44**:423-453. DOI: 10.2307/1968974

[37] Coles S. An Introduction to Statistical Modelling of Extreme Values. London: Springer-Verlag; 2001

[38] Ndlovu T, Chikobvu D. The generalised pareto distribution model approach to comparing extreme risk in the exchange rate risk of BitCoin/US Dollar and south African Rand/US Dollar returns. Risks. 2023;**11**:100. DOI: 10.3390/risks11060100

[39] Hardy MR. A regime-switching model of long-term stock returns. North American Actuarial Journal. 2001;**5**(2): 41-53

[40] Spiegelhalter DJ, Best NG, Carlin BP, Van Der Linde A. Bayesian measures of model complexity and fit. Journal of the Royal Statistical Society: Series B (Statistical Methodology). 2002; **64**(4):583-639. DOI: 10.1111/1467-9868.00353

[41] Geweke J. Bayesian inference in econometric models using Monte Carlo integration. Econometrica: Journal of the Econometric Society. 1989;**57**(6):1317-1339. DOI: 10.2307/1913710

[42] Kupiec PH. Techniques for verifying the accuracy of risk management models. Journal of Derivatives. 1995;**3** (2):73-84

Chapter 8

Evaluation of Machine Learning Algorithms and Methods for Improved Predictions in Cryptocurrency in Short-Time Horizons

Lawrence Henesey, Volodymyr Tkach, Pavlo Parkhomenko and Kiran Pingali

Abstract

Cryptocurrency has the potential to reshape financial systems and introduce financial investments that are inclusive in nature, which has led to significant research in the prediction of cryptocurrency prices by employing artificial neural networks and machine learning models. Accurate short-term predictions are essential for optimizing investment strategies, minimizing risks, and ensuring market stability. Prior studies in time-series forecasting have successfully employed statistical methods like Auto-Regressive Integrated Moving Average (ARIMA) and machine learning algorithms such as Long Short-Term Memory (LSTM). The research results presented in this paper evaluate various statistical and machine learning algorithms, assessing their accuracy and effectiveness in modeling volatile cryptocurrency data for short-term forecasting. Additionally, the study explores diverse hyperparameter settings to enhance the performance of machine learning models. The highest performance is achieved by a hybrid model combining LSTM and Deep Neural Network (DNN), showcasing its effectiveness in forecasting cryptocurrency prices with improved accuracy and capability.

Keywords: cryptocurrency, prediction, machine learning, long short-term memory (LSTM), deep neural networks

1. Introduction

Predicting the price of cryptocurrencies has become incredibly important and the ability to understand and forecast their price movements has become an area of research and analysis, leading to the use of artificial neural networks and machine learning models for this purpose. Accurate price predictions can be extremely useful in assisting investors and traders in making well-informed decisions regarding the buying and selling of cryptocurrencies. For example, Bitcoin, which skyrocketed

Figure 1.
Volatility in the price of bitcoin.

from around $10,000 in October 2020 to over $60,000 in April 2021, showcasing the potential for substantial gains or losses within short periods [1]. Precise predictions made in short-time horizons empower investors to optimize their investment strategies and minimize risks associated with market volatility. Furthermore, reliable price predictions contribute to the overall stability and maturity of the cryptocurrency market. As the market capitalization of cryptocurrencies surpassed the $2 trillion mark in April 2021 [1], their impact on the global economy has continuously grown.

Moreover, businesses accepting cryptocurrencies as a form of payment can better manage their revenues and financial planning by anticipating price fluctuations. A notable example is Tesla's decision to invest $1.5 billion in Bitcoin in early 2021, driven by the expectation of a future price increase (to provide us with more flexibility to further diversify and maximize returns on our cash) [2].

Short-term predictions are crucial in forecasting cryptocurrency prices, providing immediate insights for traders and investors. These predictions, help capitalize on short-term price movements and profit opportunities. Accurate short-term forecasts enable timely execution of buy or sell orders, optimization of trading strategies, and risk minimization for traders. Given the high volatility of cryptocurrencies, accurate short-term predictions play a vital role in maximizing returns and minimizing potential losses in this fast-paced market.

Short-term predictions can assist investors by providing insights into price movements, especially in the context of Bitcoin's volatility, as seen in **Figure 1** [3]. While Bitcoin has risk associated with it, it cannot be denied that it is an important asset. As seen in **Figure 1**, which highlights the sharp increase in the price of bitcoin between 1 January 2021 and 1 May 2021, resulting in a significant profit to its investors. Volatility affects individuals and companies that invest in Bitcoin; however, it also provides opportunities to those with proper risk management. The volatility associated with cryptocurrency makes it important to provide short-term forecasting of its price.

2. Review of published literature

Several research papers feature experiments conducted to test the accuracy of machine learning and deep learning models in making short-term predictions for time-series data. Short-term forecasting of cryptocurrency prices refers to predicting cryptocurrency prices or trends within a relatively brief time frame, typically ranging from a few seconds to a few minutes. Short-term forecasting often relies on recent data, statistical models, and real-time information to provide accurate predictions for the near future, helping to optimize operations and adapt to dynamic circumstances. Short-term forecasting usually has two approaches: statistical or machine learning.

Statistical methods and techniques based on historical data and mathematical models to make predictions, such as ARIMA, Exponential Smoothing. On the other hand, machine learning methods are approaches that leverage algorithms and computational power to learn from data and make predictions. Artificial neural networks (ANN) and random forest (RF) are common machine learning methods. For example, in [4, 5], predictions were conducted for single and multiple-time steps, revealing the LSTM model's highly suitable performance for short-term forecasting. Notably, the peak performance of the LSTM model emerged following meticulous hyperparameter tuning. Several studies pertaining to the utilization of LSTM models for short- term time series forecasting have acknowledged the importance of hyperparameter tuning in achieving model optimization [6]. There are several methods to find the optimal hyperparameters for neural networks. For example, in [7], a systematic grid search was employed to find the most suitable hyperparameter settings for LSTM models. However, it is worth noting that this grid search approach, characterized by its exhaustive exploration of hyperparameter combinations, carries a notable computational overhead. In contrast, authors in [8] discuss LSTM model optimization by manually examining and testing hyperparameter configurations.

Many studies highlight the effectiveness of ARIMA, a commonly used statistical model [5]. Although LSTM models often outperform ARIMA, ARIMA models are found to be suitable for short-term predictions as seen in [9–11]. It is important to note that while ARIMA shows satisfactory results for stationary data, it has proven to be limited in its predictive efficiency for non-stationary data as discussed in [12].

In contrast, more complex models with abilities to model the intricate dependencies in non-stationary data tend to give better results when predicting cryptocurrency prices. LSTM, and more complex neural networks like the combination of RBM-Elman model as seen in [13], convolutional neural network (CNN) with multilayer bidirectional gated recurrent unit (MB-GRU) [14], have recorded satisfactory performances for various evaluation functions [15].

It should also be noted that specifically for cryptocurrency, there can be several technical indicators that can be incorporated into the model [16, 17]. These indicators are derived from historical price, volume, or open interest data and provide insights into potential future price movements or trends. Indicators like the Relative Strength Index (RSI) and the Moving Average Convergence Divergence (MACD) measure the strength and speed of price movements. Traders use these indicators to identify overbought or oversold conditions, which may suggest a potential reversal in price. Similarly, volatility indicators like the Average True Range (ATR) can help traders gauge the potential price range in a given time frame, allowing them to set stop-loss and take-profit levels.

When applied specifically to cryptocurrency datasets, machine learning algorithms such as decision trees and XGBoost deliver promising results and lower values of root mean squared error (RMSE) [16–19]. As seen in [7], RF models give better results than LSTM, which suggests the potential for LSTM models to become overly complex and necessitate regularization. Conversely, this discrepancy might also point to a scenario wherein LSTM models, due to their simplicity, fall short in capturing the intricate underlying patterns within the data.

Additionally, machine learning algorithms such as Gated Recurrent Unit (GRU) model provides excellent results and can be considered efficient and reliable [20, 21].

The models have a scope for improvement as there can be additional feature permutation to ensure better performance by performing a sentiment analysis on social media [22, 23].

3. Research objective

Evaluating machine learning algorithms is essential to assess their reliability and effectiveness in forecasting highly volatile cryptocurrency prices, ensuring informed investment decisions. This paper reviews the performance of machine learning algorithms and statistical methods to predict the price of a cryptocurrency pair for an increasing number of time steps. The next section discusses the algorithms used, ARIMA, exponential smoothing and machine learning algorithms that explore hybrid neural network architecture of LSTM and DNN, CNN and GRU, and RF regressors. Each model explores various hyperparameter settings to fine-tune and optimize algorithm performance, aiming to achieve the best possible results. A comprehensive experimentation process was employed to train and fine-tune 72 distinct models across both LSTM-DNN and GRU-CNN architectures. The top-performing models are then compared to the best models obtained from an optimal hyperparameter search on ARIMA, exponential smoothing and RF Regressor. Evaluating these models is centered on three critical aspects: the accuracy in predicting cryptocurrency prices, the ability to model the volatile nature of the cryptocurrency prices and to sustain high performance as the number of time steps increase.

4. Methodology

4.1 Data

The datasets used to evaluate the statistical and machine learning models was provided by Fluid AI [24]. This data consisted of the ask price, the price at which a seller is willing to sell a particular cryptocurrency along with the bidding price and the time stamps for several cryptocurrency pairs. Cryptocurrency pair is a combination of two different cryptocurrency pairs that are traded against each other on a cryptocurrency exchange [25]. The forecasting models were evaluated on the dataset containing the timestamped data for the ask price specifically for the cryptocurrency pair USDT-BTC.

These datasets encompass three distinct time series, each aggregating data at different intervals: 1 second, 5 seconds, and 15 seconds. In total, all three series encompass more than 14.4 megabytes of historical data, which serves as the foundation for training the forecasting models. It's worth noting that the decision to aggregate data over 5 and 15-second intervals is strategic. Within these time intervals, discernible fluctuations in the ask price are notably pronounced, rendering them conducive for modeling and forecasting.

The visual representations below illustrate the evolution of the ask price overa one- day period. Notably, there is an initial surge, indicating a strong buying activity that propels the ask price upwards. Towards the conclusion of the day, the ask price exhibits signs of stabilization, as seen in **Figure 2**. Meanwhile, **Figure 3**, depicts the relative indicator – percentage change in Ask Price as a ratio between current price and previous subtracted by 1. This indicator allows for reducing the impact of trend and lowers the volatility level down to values that could be normalized.

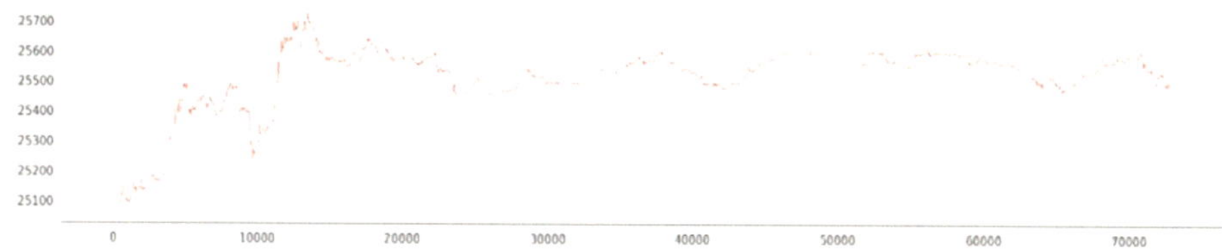

Figure 2.
Difference in ask Price for cryptocurrency pair over time.

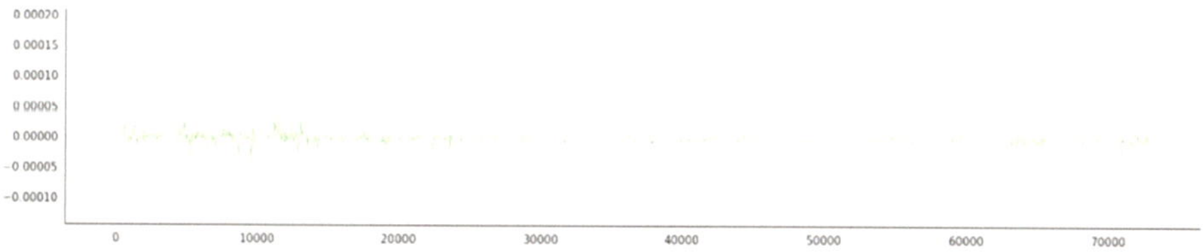

Figure 3.
Percentage change in ask Price rolling averages.

The datasets collected by FluidAI were used to train and evaluate the machine learning algorithms. Developing forecasting algorithms and executing a comprehensive hyperparameter search were conducted within the JupyterLab environment, with TensorFlow as the backbone for machine learning modeling. Furthermore, these models were validated and verified rigorously, including various computational evaluation methods and extensive discussions with the FluidAI team.

Once the datasets are loaded into the development environment, they undergo processing. The initial dataset undergoes median filtering for the ask price column. The codebase incorporates custom functions to enhance modularity and facilitate efficient data processing for future datasets. Missing values are handled through forward-fill. This is followed by adding technical cryptocurrency indicators as features to the dataset. Additionally, to enhance the modeling capability of the machine learning algorithms, several cryptocurrency technical indicators were incorporated as features in the dataset. As observed in [16], technical indicators can be grouped into five categories: Cycle indicators, momentum indicators, pattern recognition indicators, overlap study indicators, and volatility indicators. The dataset contains seven technical indicators proven effective for forecasting cryptocurrency prices [26].

This data is resampled at 1, 5, and 10-second intervals and aggregated using mean values. Features are scaled to a range between −1 and 1 using MinMaxScaler. The data is then split into training and testing datasets, and the corresponding scalers are saved for future use. Finally, the machine learning models are trained on the training data set and evaluated on the validation and test datasets. Furthermore, the machine learning models undergo an extensive hyperparameter search to aid in selecting the most optimal hyperparameters.

4.2 Forecasting models

This section investigates forecasting models trained on the cryptocurrency pair data to predict ask price. For short-term forecasting, five models were assessed. The statistical models chosen for this experiment are ARIMA and Simple Exponential Smoothing. ARIMA model captures and forecasts patterns in time series data by considering its autoregressive behavior, differencing to achieve stationarity, and accounting for moving average effects. In ARIMA the Autoregressive component models the relationship between the current data point and previous data points in the series. It signifies that a time series's current value can depend on its past values [27]. In contrast to ARIMA, Exponential Smoothing assigns exponentially decreasing weights to past observations, giving more importance torecent data.

Exponential smoothing methods have been widely researched and are considered powerful for certain types of time series data, especially when the data exhibits trends and seasonality [28]. This paper evaluates the Simple Exponential Smoothing model. ARIMA model was tuned with 108 hyperparameter settings and the hyperparameters were chosen with a focus to find the optimal values of p (Autoregressive Order), q (Moving Average Order) and d (Integrated Order). ARIMA was tuned separately for all three series of the dataset. Similarly, the Simple Exponential Smoothing model was trained over 100 values of the hyperparameter alpha. To obtain the best model for all three series that predict ask price at different time intervals (1, 5 and 15) in the future, a grid search in conjunction with a rolling cross-validation split were used to optimize the hyperparameters.

The two statistical models are compared to an RF model, LSTM-DNN and CNN-GRU models. LSTM model is a Recurrent Neural Network (RNN) type that can effectively capture long-range dependencies in the past in contrast to RNN. This is because of its ability to avoid the vanishing gradient problem that occurs during RNN learning [29]. LSTMs can capture and remember long-term dependencies and patterns in sequential data. They do this through a combination of mechanisms, including cell state, three gates and hidden state.

The model developed to be evaluated in this paper is a hybrid neural network consisting of LSTM and DNN. Several studies have been conducted to assess the effectiveness of LSTM in short-term forecasting and for this reason LSTM was chosen. Moreover, DNNs are excellent at automatically learning hierarchical representations of data. Combining LSTM with DNN layers allows the network to extract complex and abstract features from the time series data, potentially capturing patterns and dependencies that may be challenging for LSTM alone. The normalization was applied to data in all three series to improve performance. The normalization does not significantly help the model to forecast, however it is necessary to improve the results when dealing with high values. To obtain the best model, a hyperparameter search was performed with the following hyperparameters:

- The number of LSTM layers because the choice of the number of layers can have a significant impact on the network's performance and its ability to capture underlying patterns in data. The hyperparameter selection for the number of LSTM layers included values of 1, 2, and 4. This range was chosen to mitigate issues such as overfitting, gradient explosion as the number of layers is stacked and to reduce the need for extensive regularization techniques [30].

- The number of DNN layers that are added in the network as the output layer. The hyperparameter selection for the number of DNN layers included values of 1 and 2. This range ensures that fewer parameters and computations are required, making the network less prone to memorizing noise in the data [31].

- The optimization algorithm as it influences the training and performance of machine learning algorithms. The hyperparameter selection encompassed adaptive (Adam and RMSProp) and non-adaptive (Stochastic Gradient Descent) optimization algorithms. These algorithms were then trained and tested on various learning rates [31].

The hyperparameter settings mentioned above generated 72 models for each time series and a total of 216 models overall. The table below (**Table 1**) shows the Mean Squared Error obtained after the hyperparameter tuning of the LSTM-DNN models for a learning rate of 0.01.

It was observed that the optimal hyperparameter configuration for the model comprised a single layer of LSTM and a corresponding DNN layer, utilizing the Adam optimization algorithm. Additionally, it was also observed that the choice of optimization algorithm significantly influenced the convergence time for each model. Similarly, another hybrid neural network was trained and tuned to identify the optimal network architecture. This combination was developed using CNN and GRU layers. GRU is a type of RNN that is used in deep learning for sequential data tasks, such as natural language processing and time series analysis. GRUs are a variation of

	MSE		
Hyperparameter	**1 second**	**5 seconds**	**10 seconds**
(Number of LSTM layers, Number of DNN layers, Optimization Algorithm)			
1, 1, Adam	0.02841	0.21587	0.23102
1, 2, Adam	0.02372	0.35312	**0.13236**
2, 2, Adam	0.02168	0.33236	0.26504
2, 1, Adam	0.02023	0.30567	0.23451
4, 1, Adam	0.02367	0.45231	0.45321
4, 2, Adam	0.02190	0.44675	0.44765
1, 1, RMSProp	**0.01707**	**0.17234**	0.32765
1, 2, RMSProp	0.01986	0.31565	0.38455
2, 2, RMSProp	0.01774	0.20745	0.41321
2, 1, RMSProp	0.02331	0.25678	0.56234
4, 1, RMSProp	0.02578	0.38346	0.67321
4, 2, RMSProp	0.02445	0.40123	0.56225
1, 1, SGD	0.02072	0.18766	0.18743
1, 2, SGD	0.01739	0.19312	0.19611
2, 1, SGD	0.03173	0.43388	0.34213
2, 2, SGD	0.02177	0.34377	0.44218
4, 1, SGD	0.02208	0.48932	0.47678
4, 2, SGD	0.02245	0.47752	0.53126

Table 1.
Mean squared error for LSTM-DNN with a learning rate of 0.01.

the more traditional LSTM (Long Short-Term Memory) networks and were designed to address some of the computational complexities associated with LSTMs. Like LSTMs, GRUs have gating mechanisms that allow them to selectively update and reset their hidden states. GRUs have a simplified structure compared to LSTMs. They have two gates, an update gate and a reset gate and they do not have a separate memory cell like LSTMs. Instead, they use the hidden state to store and update information from previous time steps. In this paper, a combination of CNN and GRU is assessed because CNNs excel at extracting spatial features and patterns from sequential data which can then be processed by GRUs to capture temporal dependencies. This would lead to robust model, effective for complex time series patterns. The hyperparameter settings used for the CNN-GRU are identical to the LSTM-DNN model and lead to 72 models for each time series and a cumulative of 216 models. The table below (**Table 2**) depicts the Mean Squared Error recorded for all hyperparameter settings used for the CNN-GRU neural network with a learning rate of 0.01.

The optimal forecasting model consisted of a single GRU layer with two layers of CNN utilizing the Adam optimization algorithm. The statistical models and the neural networks are finally compared to each other and an RF Model. The forecasting model for RF is enhanced by conducting a grid search to make the best choices for the following parameters:

	MSE		
Hyperparameter	**1 second**	**5 seconds**	**10 seconds**
(Number of GRU layers, Number of DNN layers, Optimization Algorithm)			
1, 1, Adam	0.0683	**0.3038**	**0.2229**
1, 2, Adam	0.0939	0.4558	0.4886
2, 2, Adam	0.1031	0.5263	0.6579
2, 1, Adam	0.1030	0.5732	0.7396
4, 1, Adam	0.0992	0.6114	0.7734
4, 2, Adam	0.0942	0.6443	0.7826
1, 1, RMSProp	0.0892	0.6726	0.7795
1, 2, RMSProp	0.0845	0.6967	0.7702
2, 2, RMSProp	0.0805	0.7168	0.7580
2, 1, RMSProp	0.0771	0.7332	0.7447
4, 1, RMSProp	0.0742	0.7465	0.7312
4, 2, RMSProp	0.0718	0.7569	0.7180
1, 1, SGD	0.0698	0.7650	0.7055
1, 2, SGD	0.0682	0.7711	0.6937
2, 1, SGD	0.0668	0.7755	0.6828
2, 2, SGD	0.0656	0.7787	0.6727
4, 1, SGD	0.0647	0.7807	0.6633
4, 2, SGD	**0.0638**	0.7819	0.6548

Table 2.
Mean squared error for CNN-GRU with a learning rate of 0.01.

DOI: http://dx.doi.org/10.5772/intechopen.1004320

- The number of decision trees. Tuning the model lead to 50 decision trees for the best forecasting model.
- The maximum depth. This was recorded as 10 for the optimal forecasting model.

4.3 Evaluation methods

The forecasting models were evaluated by comparing the results obtained with a few well-known approaches. To better understand the errors, Mean Squared Error (MSE) was used as a measure of the prediction. The error can be expressed as:

$$MSE = \frac{1}{n}\sum_{i=1}^{n}\left(Y_i - \hat{Y}_i\right)^2 \quad (1)$$

Here n is the number of observations, Y_i corresponds to the forecast value $\hat{Y}_i$ is the actual value. The performance evaluation was carried out on the test set comprising the most recent 30% data entries. Prediction accuracy was evaluated for all three time series.

Moreover, visualizations were generated to facilitate a visual assessment of alignment and to detect potential anomalies in the time series predictions. While comparing the models with each other, another metric, MSE Percentage Reduction is used. MSE Percentage Reduction is a metric used to quantify the improvement in model performance when comparing two different models or scenarios. It calculates the percentage decrease in the MSE between baseline and improved models. The result is expressed as a percentage, indicating the reduction in MSE achieved by moving from the baseline to the improved model. A higher Percentage MSE Reduction indicates a more significant improvement in model accuracy, with a reduction of 100% indicating that the improved model has completely eliminated the errors compared to the baseline.

Additionally, an evaluation metric called 'hit ratio' is used to evaluate the performance of each model individually. The hit ratio is a percentage representing the proportion of correct predictions or successful trades out of the total number of predictions.

5. Research results

The outcomes obtained from both, the five models and the hyperparameter tuning process, which was conducted to refine the models. These results collectively guided the selection of the optimal model. **Table 3** shows the hit ratio obtained for each machine-learning model.

The analysis of **Tables 3** and **4** reveals that LSTM-DNN consistently exhibits superior performance compared to the other four models. Furthermore, it is noteworthy that, with increasing time steps, a decline in performance becomes apparent, although CNN-GRU maintains remarkable stability across all time steps. Additionally, while statistical methods outperform RF, it is evident that when compared with neural networks, they exhibit a lower prediction accuracy.

LSTM has a percentage reduction in MSE of approximately 19.86% compared to ARIMA. This indicates that LSTM's predictions are roughly 19.86% closer to

ML model	HIT ratio		
	1 second	5 seconds	10 seconds
ARIMA	68.1%	59%	58.5%
EXP-SMOOTHING	64.5%	22.5%	45.2%
LSTM-DNN	**83.2%**	**78.4%**	**66%**
CNN-GRU	72.8%	70.6%	63.2%
RF	57.9%	31.2%	36.8%

Table 3.
Hit ratio per model for cryptocurrency prices at 1, 5 and 15 second intervals.

ML model	MSE		
	1 second	5 seconds	10 seconds
ARIMA	0.021683	0.094553	0.094556
EXP-SMOOTHING	0.035761	0.771107	0.448823
LSTM-DNN	**0.017398**	**0.017534**	**0.019236**
CNN-GRU	0.020843	0.038410	0.022976
RF	0.267892	0.564218	0.678322

Table 4.
MSE per model for cryptocurrency prices at 1, 5 and 15 second intervals.

the actual values than ARIMA's predictions, providing a percentage-based measure of the improvement in predictive accuracy. Additionally, when compared to Exponential.

Smoothing, LSTM has a percentage reduction of approximately is 51.31%. This is because ARIMA and Exponential Smoothing models are based on linear or exponential relationships, limiting their ability to capture the complex, non-linear patterns often seen in cryptocurrency price data. ARIMA models are most effective when applied to stationary time series data. Stationarity implies that statistical properties like mean, and variance remain constant over time. ARIMA models are designed to capture and predict patterns in stationary data by modeling the autoregressive, differencing, and moving average components. However, since this time series data is non-stationary, meaning it exhibits trends, seasonality, or other changing statistical properties, ARIMA models do not perform well. Meanwhile, LSTM excels at modeling intricate dependencies in sequential data.

Interestingly, all models exhibit strong performance at a one-second interval, with LSTM-DNN standing out. Additionally, it is also be observed that the LSTM-DNN performs well in the training and test phases and shows good generalization abilities as seen in **Figure 4**. Observations reveal that models like LSTM-DNN (as seen in **Figure** 5) and CNN-GRU tend to overfit with an increase in the number of LSTM and GRU layers, which leads to less accurate predictions. Notably, performance is a noticeable deterioration as the time period extends. This could be overcome by regularization techniques, such as using dropout layers.

RF models exhibit subpar generalization, even with an exhaustive hyperparameter search. Notably, the best-performing RF model consistently underperforms when

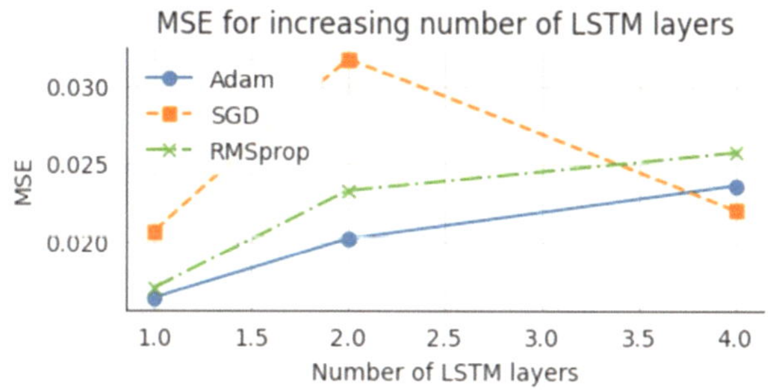

Figure 4.
MSE for varying number of LSTM layers.

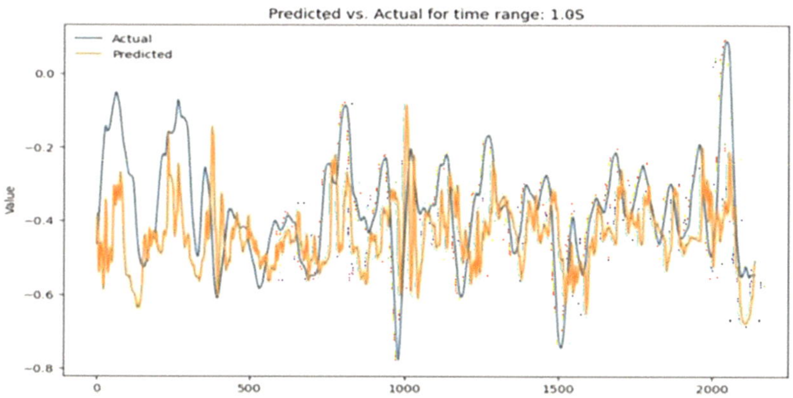

Figure 5.
Comparison of normalized actual & predicted values of cryptocurrency pair at one-second intervals measured for relative indicators (as a ratio between current and previous value). LSTM-DNN.

compared to ARIMA. This could be due to their lack of temporal understanding, difficulty in handling non-stationarity, and limited historical context. Moreover, it should be noted that RF is sensitive to hyperparameters, data transformation requirements, and faces challenges in capturing seasonality and trends. Focusing on the CNN-GRU models results in better performance when compared to statistical methods.

However, GRU models have fewer parameters and may struggle to capture and remember long-term trends effectively in contrast to LSTM. Additionally, cryptocurrency markets are highly volatile and can exhibit sudden, unpredictable changes, which LSTM's longer memory can help capture, making them more suitable for this specific forecasting task.

6. Conclusion

The results from the research study that was conducted feature a comparative analysis of five machine learning algorithms for cryptocurrency price forecasting while identifying optimal hyperparameters for each model. The notably high hit ratio of 83.2% as seen in **Table 3**, and substantial MSE Percentage Reduction achieved by the LSTM-DNN model underscore its performance in this dataset. It's worth emphasizing that accurate cryptocurrency price prediction demands a robust model capable of capturing market trends effectively which lead to the development of a hybrid neural network which was verified and tested.

Future work and improvements would include augmenting the dataset with additional technical indicators, expanding its size, and considering longer-term trends. Furthermore, integrating sentiment analysis into predictive models could enhance accuracy. Notably, the research indicates potential cross-pair forecasting, where models trained on one cryptocurrency pair yield reliable predictions forothers. Development of more robust prediction systems is possible by further work and research by combining various models. It is also important to note that models trained to predict based on MSE while having a low error in the predictions might not possess comparable level of prediction power, since a very simple trailing prediction model – "repeat the previous value" – may have the lowest MSE possible, whilst simply trailing the original price chart and having no prediction power.

Author details

Lawrence Henesey[1,2]*, Volodymyr Tkach[2,3,4], Pavlo Parkhomenko[2] and Kiran Pingali[2]

1 Blekinge Institute of Technology, Karlshamn, Sweden

2 Fluid AI, fluidai.com, New York, USA

3 Igor Sikorsky Kyiv Polytechnic Institute, Kyiv, Ukraine

4 George Mason University, Fairfax, VA, USA

*Address all correspondence to: lhe@bth.se

References

[1] CoinMarketCap. Cryptocurrency Market Capitalizations. Available from: https://coinmarketcap.com/

[2] Tesla. Form 10-K. 2021. Available from: https://www.sec.gov/ix?doc=/Archives/edgar/data/1318605/000156459021004599/tsla-10k_20201231.htm

[3] Sigalos M. Bitcoin's wild price moves stem from its design—you'll need strong nerves to trade it [Internet]. CNBC; 2021. Available from: https://www.cnbc.com/2021/05/19/why-is-bitcoin-so-volatile.html

[4] Liu Y, Wang Y, Yang X, Zhang L. Short-term travel time prediction by deep learning: A comparison of different LSTM-DNN models. In: 2017 IEEE 20th International Conference on Intelligent Transportation Systems (ITSC). Yokohama, Japan: IEEE; Oct 2017:16-19. pp. 1-8. DOI: 10.1109/ITSC.2017.8317886

[5] Masum S, Liu Y, Chiverton J. Multi-step time series forecasting of electric load using machine learning models. In: Artificial Intelligence and Soft Computing: 17th International Conference, ICAISC 2018, June 3-7, 2018, Zakopane, Poland, Proceedings, Part I 17. Cham, Switzerland: Springer International; 2018. pp. 148-159. (Lecture Notes in Computer Science; Vol. 10841). DOI: 10.1007/978-3-319.91253-0_15

[6] Hochreiter S, Schmidhuber J. Long short-term memory. Neural Computation. 1997;**9**(8):1735-1780

[7] Toqué F, Khouadjia M, Come E, Trepanier M, Oukhellou L. Short & long term forecasting of multimodal transport passenger flows with machine learning methods. In: 2017 IEEE 20th International Conference on Intelligent Transportation Systems (ITSC). Yokohama, Japan: IEEE; Oct 2017:6-19. 2017. pp. 560-566. DOI: 10.1109/ITSC40621.2017

[8] Yadav A, Jha CK, Sharan A. Optimizing LSTM for time series prediction in Indian stock market. Procedia Computer Science. 2020;**167**:2091-2100

[9] Meyler A, Kenny G, Quinn T. Forecasting Irish Inflation Using ARIMA Models. Dublin, Ireland: Central Bank of Ireland; 1998. pp. 1-48

[10] Ahmed MS, Cook AR. Analysis of Freeway Traffic Time-Series Data by Using Box-Jenkins Techniques. 1979. (No. 722)

[11] Billings D, Yang JS. Application of the ARIMA models to urban roadway travel time prediction-a case study. In: 2006 IEEE International Conference on Systems, Man and Cybernetics. Vol. 3. Piscataway, New Jersey, USA: IEEE; 2006. pp. 2529-2534. DOI: 10.1109/ICSMC.2006.385244

[12] Wang S, Li C, Lim A. Why are the ARIMA and SARIMA not sufficient. 2019:1-15, arXiv abs/1904.07632. [Accessed: March 3, 2024]

[13] Zhang X, Wang R, Zhang T, Liu Y, Zha Y. Short-term load forecast- ing using a novel deep learning framework. Energies. 2018;**11**(6):1554

[14] Khan ZA, Ullah A, Ullah W, Rho S, Lee M, Baik SW. Electrical energy prediction in residential buildings for short-term horizons using hybrid deep learning strategy. Applied Sciences. 2020;**10**(23):8634

[15] Weerakody PB, Wong KW, Wang G, Ela W. A review of irregular time series data handling with gated recurrent neural networks. Neurocomputing. 2021;**441**:161-178

[16] Huang JZ, Huang W, Ni J. Predicting bitcoin returns using high-dimensional technical indicators. The Journal of Finance and Data Science. 2019;**5**(3):140-155

[17] Wilder JW. New Concepts in Technical Trading Systems. Tucson, Arizona, USA: Trend Research; 1978 ISBN 9780894590276

[18] Iqbal M, Iqbal M, Jaskani F, Iqbal K, Hassan A. Time-series prediction of cryptocurrency market using machine learning techniques. EAI Endorsed Transactions on Creative Technologies. 2021;**8**(28)

[19] Jaquart P, Dann D, Weinhardt C. Short-term bitcoin market prediction via machine learning. The journal of finance and data science. 2021;**7**:45-66

[20] Faraji M, Nadi S, Ghaffarpasand O, Homayoni S, Downey K. An integrated 3D CNN-GRU deep learning method for short-term prediction of PM2. 5 concentration in urban environment. Science of the Total Environment. 2022;**834**:155324

[21] Li C, Tang G, Xue X, Saeed A, Hu X. Short-term wind speed interval prediction based on ensemble GRU model. IEEE Transactions on Sustainable Energy. 2019;**11**(3):1370-1380

[22] Hamayel MJ, Owda AY. A novel cryptocurrency price prediction model using GRU, LSTM and bi-LSTM machine learning algorithms. AI. 2021;**2**(4):477-496

[23] Su Y, Kuo CCJ. On extended long short-term memory and dependent bidirectional recurrent neural network. Neurocomputing. 2019;**356**:151-161

[24] FluidAI - Liquidity Aggregation Platform for Retail and Institutional Crypto Trading [Internet]. FluidAI; 2023 [Accessed: December 12, 2023]. Available from: https://fluidai.com/

[25] Maiti M, Vukovic D, Krakovich V, Pandey MK. How integrated are cryptocurrencies. International Journal of Big Data Management. 2020;**1**(1):64-80

[26] Alonso-MonsalveS,Suárez-CetruloAL, Cervantes A, Quintana D. Convolution on neural networks for high-frequency trend prediction of cryptocurrency exchange rates using technical indicators. Expert Systems with Applications. 2020;**149**:113250

[27] Shumway RH, Stoffer DS, Shumway RH, Stoffer DS. ARIMA models. Time series analysis and its applications: With R examples. In: Shumway RH, Stoffer DS, editors. Springer Texts in Statistics. Cham, Switzerland: Springer International Publishing; 2017. pp. 75-163. ISBN: 978-3-319-52451-1

[28] De Livera AM, Hyndman RJ, Snyder RD. Forecasting time series with complex seasonal patterns using exponential smoothing. Journal of the Ameri- can statistical association. 2011;**106**(496):1513-1527

[29] Sherstinsky A. Fundamentals of recurrent neural network (RNN) and long short-term memory (LSTM) network. Physica D: Nonlinear Phenomena. 2020;**404**:132306

[30] Merity S, Keskar NS, Socher R. Regularizing and optimizing LSTM language models. 2017:1-10, arXiv:1708.02182 [Accessed: March 3, 2024]

[31] Shubha SS, Sen T, Shen H, Normansell M. A diverse noise- resilient DNN ensemble model on edge devices for time-series data. In: 2021 18th Annual IEEE International Conference on Sensing, Communication, and Networking (SECON) 6-9 July 2021 as a Virtual Conference. Piscataway, New Jersey, USA: IEEE; 2021. pp. 1-9. DOI: 10.1109/SECON52354.2021.9491607